# Life on Earth II

## "Delusions of Tiny"

By

Chris Hallinger

Cover painting of Chris, Carol, Fluffy and Recumbent Bike

By John Schirmer

Accomac Press

Fairfield, Iowa

Accomac Press
209 N. 9th Street
Fairfield, Iowa 52556
Accomacpress.com
Copyright 2015

All rights reserved. No part of this book may be reproduced or utilized in any form or by any means, electronic or mechanical, including photocopying, recording or by information storage and retrieval system, without permission from the publisher.

Please purchase only authorized electronic editions. Your support of author's rights is appreciated.

ISBN: 978-0-9846738-4-1

1. Humor
2. Memoir
3. Philadelphia
4. Landlord
5. The Peppermint Twist

## Acknowledgements — A Big "Thank You" to:

Carol Olicker for great editing work, and many years of thrills and spills.

John Schirmer for the cover painting of the author with Carol and recumbent bike, at the reservoir. Find him online at www.schirmerwoodcuts.com

Paul Delisle for photo, computer and website work.

Kristina Creighton for publishing and editing advice. Check out her *Kristina's Kitchen Cookbook*.

Cathy Matt for editing help, and Chinese lunches.

Linda Hallinger for editing, support and aloha vibes.

*In memory of David "Dog" Hallinger*

# Contents

A Life of Hardships ............................................................... 1

Coal into Diamonds .............................................................. 4

Niagara Falls ........................................................................ 7

What the Hay ..................................................................... 10

Fear Is Important ............................................................... 13

The Golf Ball Factory Fire ................................................. 16

Schmuck with an Underwood .......................................... 19

Money Talks ....................................................................... 22

An Audience Experience ................................................... 25

What to Say ........................................................................ 29

A Sales Pitch ....................................................................... 32

Snowflakes Are Our Friends ............................................. 35

Being Sick, It's a Part of Life ............................................. 39

An Experiment in Terror ................................................... 42

Shooting Stars .................................................................... 45

What Happened to Potter? ............................................... 48

The Magic Tube .................................................................. 52

What the Guys are Saying ................................................ 56

Hash Songs ......................................................................... 59

We Need the Funnies ........................................................ 62

Two Screenplays ................................................................ 65

High School Sweethearts ............................................................... 68
What did Betty Do? ....................................................................... 71
Life Review .................................................................................... 75
We Have Been to Europe ............................................................. 79
Headline News ............................................................................... 83
On the Beach ................................................................................. 86
Altered States ................................................................................ 89
The Green Falcon ......................................................................... 92
Honey Goes Blind ........................................................................ 96
All You Can Eat .......................................................................... 100
The Wyncote Olympics ............................................................. 103
The Five Gottas .......................................................................... 107
Bud's Lottery Dream ................................................................. 110
Of Mice and Women ................................................................. 113
Two Dogs Saved My Life ......................................................... 116
The Rooming House .................................................................. 119
The Black Couch ........................................................................ 122
Hamstring Muscles ................................................................... 125
Watching for Fires ..................................................................... 128
Memorial for the Dog ............................................................... 131
Dog's Life in Photos .................................................................. 134
The Pilgrimage ........................................................................... 139
First Openly Gay Tuba Player ................................................. 142

"I am but one grain of sand. But if I were to be moved, all the other grains of sand would shift."

    --sign on my mother's desk

"Never stand between a Republican and his gun, or a Democrat and his recycling bin."

    --sign in a political campaign office

"Hippies: Use Side Door."

    --sign on a saloon door in Wyoming

# **A Life of Hardships**

You young people of today, as if there were any reading this book, would not believe what life was like in the olden days (1950-1959). Life was hard, everything was difficult, and suffering was normal. Things you take for granted didn't exist.

If we were out riding our bikes, there was no way for us to get a phone call. Nobody could text us. A text was a gigantic book that we had to lug back and forth to school. There wasn't a video game in sight. The only reality we had was reality.

We had to walk to school in a half inch of snow. Then we had to learn things. One year I had to make a list of all the books I had read that year. Since I hadn't read any books, I had to make up some titles. One was A *Life of Hardships* by Stone. I couldn't come up with a first name, so the author's name was just "Stone."

This book told the story of a pioneer family trying to survive against untold obstacles. I couldn't think of any obstacles, so they were untold. The family perseveres in the end, and just as the sun is setting, they are putting up some preserves. It's enough to make you cry. My teacher knew there was no such book, but she let it go. Now *A Life of Hardships* actually exists, as a chapter in this book. Truth is stranger than fiction.

Junior high was a tough place. We had to use lockers, take typing and industrial arts, and pretend we were learning Spanish (try faking *that*). And if that wasn't enough, we also had to go to dances. This is a time of change and stress. After junior high, everything starts getting easier. Kids, I thought you should know that.

Then later in the 1960's, the hippie revolution happened. Haircuts, shaving, and careers all became optional. People traveled across the country by thumb. You could just walk to the nearest curb and start hitchhiking. There were thousands of people traveling that way. You'd see them everywhere, and it all seemed normal.

If you tried to do that today, you'd be picked up by a mass murderer who was trying to fill his monthly quota. This takes the fun right out of it, so hitchhiking went out of style. Everybody gave up being hippies. Now the only thing that matters is being a success.

So what is the secret of a successful life? You're asking the wrong guy. If I knew, would I be sitting here trying to write this book? No, I would be next to the pool in one of those reclining chairs. Most people who write about how to be a success have never been one.

It's a tough life down here on earth. You have to come up with some kind of scheme. Some people have theirs all figured out in kindergarten. Then they actually follow through, the whole thing comes true, and they end up relaxed and happy. Others of us are still looking.

My latest idea is The Museum of Broken Flashlights. We have an enormous collection of them, in all colors and sizes, lying around the house. We need to form them into a collection, label them, and set up a ticket booth. Carol can run the snack bar. Then it's just a matter of collecting the money.

This museum will be a big hit. Someday there will be a sign on Route 80 saying "Exit here for Flashlight Museum." Wives will say to their husbands, "Let's stop here, honey." Husbands will reply, "No way. We have to make it to Colorado by nightfall." The next thing he knows, he'll be pulling into our driveway for the complete tour.

Later we can expand our exhibit to include The Hall of Pens that Don't Write. We have enough of those to fill a museum, and then some extras to start a few franchises. Your town could probably use one. I'm just saying.

## Coal into Diamonds

When we were little kids, back in the day, we tried to make diamonds from coal. We heard that diamonds were made from pressurized coal, so we decided to speed up the process with a hammer and a little elbow grease. We spent the afternoon smashing coal out on the cement patio.

We were young entrepreneurs, and we knew how to set goals and work towards them. We had a plan for early retirement. Why not retire at age 6? Why not skip the whole school, still more school, bizarre career, crazy co-workers thing that everybody has to go through?

Why not pound a little coal and become tot millionaires overnight? Not even overnight. Same day! I would call this sound financial thinking and good life planning. We didn't need to see a prospectus or talk to any advisors. We knew a good idea when we thought of it.

I'm not sure who came up with the plan. We were sitting there one Saturday morning, watching cartoons and eating bowls of sugar with a few corn flakes mixed in. The day stretched out in front of us, with all its possibilities, such as watching more cartoons and eating lunch. Suddenly somebody had the brainstorm, and we swung into action.

We figured this was a good summer project, with more potential than a lemonade stand. Even if we just made 20 or 30 diamonds, that would be a good day's haul. Our dogs came out to join us, but they soon lost interest and wandered off. Dogs are hard to understand.

We got the original concept for this project from Superman comics, because most of what we knew came from comic books. Superman would occasionally squeeze a lump of coal to make a diamond for his gal, Lois Lane. We could do the same thing, but keep the final products for ourselves. Pretty straight-forward business plan. Any banker would agree.

There were very few start-up costs. The hammer already existed, down in the cellar. The coal was right there in the same room. We had a coal furnace in those days. A guy with a big truck backed into our driveway, raised the back of his truck, and a few tons of coal slid down a metal chute right into the coal bin. We grabbed a few handfuls of coal, which we now thought of as black gold, or Texas tea.

Then we laid the coal out, and pounded for all we were worth. Mostly we made little coal pieces and a big mess. Our clothes got dirty, and so did our hands and faces. A major clean-up was needed. The patio was also a wreck. You have to get your hands dirty if you want to get anywhere in this world.

We also experimented with charcoal, which we borrowed from the outdoor grill. That didn't hold well under hammer pounding. It went right into dust mode, and there it stayed. Even Superman couldn't have done much with charcoal.

The frustrating part was, we knew the diamonds were in there, hiding from us, just out of reach. We just couldn't hit the coal hard enough. We were motivated, young Horatio Algers. We pounded for all we were worth. We wanted to be rich, and we were not ashamed.

In the end, we hardly made any diamonds. OK, we made zero. But at least we tried. We had ambition in those days. We wanted to get somewhere in life, not just keep up with the Joneses, but go flying past them in our limos, flooring it, so the gravel sprayed in their faces. We wanted to be kings and queens for a day, with new Schwinn bikes and all the sodas we could drink. Was that asking too much?

Apparently it was. We found out the hard way why so many rich folks are anti-science. Science gets in the way of profit. If it weren't for the laws of science, we really would have hit it big, with our hammers.

# Niagara Falls

When we were little kids, my parents took us on sightseeing trips, so we could practice yelling at each other in the back of a station wagon. One place we went was Niagara Falls.

We stayed in a motel up the river from the falls. They had nice bedrooms with TVs, and an ice machine in the hall. If you bought a soda, you could have ice. That is luxury.

We saw the falls from every possible angle, above and below, at night and in daylight, from land and from sea. We took an elevator up a big tower and looked down on them. We stood behind railings at the edge of the falls, and resisted the urge to jump in.

This might remind you of the movie *Niagara* with Marilyn Monroe. In the end the bad guy goes over the falls in a speedboat. He doesn't survive, and neither does the boat. The man was evil, but everybody felt bad about the boat.

We also saw the falls from Canada. This was our first trip to a foreign country. We didn't need shots, passports, or quinine tablets. They are pretty much like us over there, except they put vinegar on their French fries. You can tell a lot about another culture by the way they treat their French fries. On our return trip we had to talk to a really stern American guy in a uniform, who asked us just what in the world did we think we were doing? Nothing, we all said. He seemed satisfied with the answer and eventually let us back into the states.

Also we saw the falls from the deck of the USS *Maid of the Mist*. This is an old WWII destroyer that somehow made it up the Niagara River and is on duty there. She fired off a few depth charges for our amusement. We drove up so close to the falls that we were hit by the spray. They gave us yellow raincoats to wear, but we had to give them back.

We saw the falls from underneath, on a slippery wooden walkway, with constant spray making it really slick and waterlogged, but luckily the walkway was protected with Thompsons® Water Sealer. We also got behind the falls, in a secret tunnel that the FBI doesn't know about.

Then we went to some museums that told the history of the falls, and the folks who tried to go over them in barrels and other homemade projectiles. Some of them lived. They all had one thing in common: they were crazy.

The first one was an elderly woman with her cat. They both survived, but the cat never spoke to her again. There was a guy who went over with his turtle but only the turtle made it. Turtles are built for that kind of thing; people not so much.

There was one guy who put a pile of inner tubes around himself. He added a layer of fishnet around that, for extra safety. Two days later they found a piece of fishnet downstream, and a note to his wife saying: "Honey, I forgot to take the chicken out of the freezer. Please forgive me."

Then there were the two guys who went over together in a barrel. When they came out of the hatch, they were wearing cowboy hats, and not much else. What happens in the barrel stays in the barrel.

OK! We also tried out the plunge-o-simulator, which imitates the actual experience of going over Niagara Falls in a barrel. We sat on facing benches, and the lights went out. Some water sound effects came out of a speaker, and the benches shook. Then the lights came back on and the benches stopped shaking. The ride was over. Nothing to do now but get some souvenirs.

We also saw the falls at night. Spotlights made them look red, white, and blue, and we felt patriotic. Then a green light came on, and we didn't know what to feel.

There is a big dam in that area where they make electricity, which is sold by the hour to needy citizens downstate along with plastic Niagara Falls ashtrays. This concludes my memories of Niagara Falls.

## **What the Hay**

One soggy Iowa day, I stood on the back step and looked out at the rain coming down in my "yard," which is in quotes because it is really just a patch of dirt surrounded by a fence. I can't get grass to grow there. I tried many times. I scraped up the soil, put on a package of grass seed, and covered it with straw.

Is it hay or straw? I think it is straw. A quick check of the Internet will bring the answer. (Some minutes pass. The author abandons you. Be brave.) Well, guess what? I spent some time reading the differences between hay and straw, and I still don't know the answer. It must be one or the other. Try not to worry about it.

Many years ago, I'm talking about the old days, when people were smart and phones were dumb; our family went to live on a farm for a week. This was a new idea my mother had. She wanted us to do chores, plow the earth, feed the cattle—the whole rural experience.

We were from the suburbs. There were no crops on our land, and not a subsidy in sight. There was an old horse stable next to the garage, but the horses were long gone. My older sister converted part of the stable into a bomb shelter; in case the area became radioactive, which was a real possibility back then. Like so many other times, those times were difficult.

We had a small tractor that was used for cutting the grass. You couldn't plow a field or harvest the corn with it. It came with a few attachments, but none were for plowing or harvesting crops. My mother wanted us to try genuine farm life to see what it was like.

We went to a special farm that accepted guests. We had dinners with the family around a big table. We patted the dog and scratched his ears as needed. He was a pup of the soil, an honest working dog who helped out and did what he was told.

We all helped out with the chores. Looking back on it, this was a good deal for the farm family. They got some free help, but you have to wonder how much help a bunch of little kids were. One chore we did was to help bring bales of hay into the barn. They went up a big conveyor belt and we climbed up and helped throw them into place. The air was full of hay particles.

What my brother and I had forgotten, in the excitement of the moment, was that we both had serious hay fever problems. That night neither of us could breathe, like the guy in *Total Recall* who gets plopped down on Mars and is gasping away while his eyeballs popped out in a comical way.

I was sneezing like a fool, nonstop, for hours. My eyes were swollen shut. I looked like the bad guy in *Dirty Harry* who paid to have himself beaten up. My brother had such a hard time breathing that we wondered if the hospital might be needed. Somehow we survived.

It was an eventful week. One day the family dog was run over by the big cart that goes behind the tractor. He lived through it and took the rest of the day off. Another time we rounded up a herd of 77 sheep and moved them from one field to another. We ran around yelling at the sheep and clapping our hands. It turns out that sheep will follow instructions if you accompany them with clapping and yelling. Then we had some lemonade. This was the good life.

*One bad thing happened on that farm trip. I wet the bed. I wasn't supposed to because I was pretty old by then, but for various personal reasons I was still wetting the bed at an advanced age. This caused many problems in situations like this. What was the matter with me? Trained psychologists gave it their best shot, but couldn't figure out the cause. The farmer's wife wasn't happy about her stained sheets. It was a dark day. Maybe you should skip this paragraph. Shoot, too late now.*

Anyway, I looked out over the "yard," which still doesn't have grass in it, in the pouring rain. That's the truth. Telling hard truths is what writing is all about. Later somebody reads these truths and they get depressed for a while. It's a good system.

# **Fear Is Important**

Fear is an important emotion. It gets you out of bed and moving in the morning, and puts the cut in your stride. The problem is, it also stops you from doing a lot of good things. Being chicken is a big part of life.

When I was growing up, there was a song we used to sing that had to do with fear, called "I'm Chicken." The words are "I'm chicken, I'm chicken, I'm chicken, peck, peck, peck." You had to make a pecking motion on your hand with each peck. We sang that song a lot, because we were afraid of a lot of things, and I was the biggest chicken of them all. I was scared of a whole list of things, including:

**The Dark**. I wouldn't go to sleep at night unless the lamp was on. The lamp had to stay on all night, with the door open. Even then, I had to read comic books to help me relax and fall asleep. I read the same comic books over and over for years. Mostly Archies, with a few Caspers and Little Lulu's. I had them memorized, even the ads for the civil war soldiers on realistic plastic bases. Comic books can bring great comfort, and that's why they were invented. We tried to get the dogs to come and sleep with us but it didn't happen. They usually hung around the big folks who worked the can opener.

**The Twilight Zone.** Every Friday night we watched the *Twilight Zone,* and then I was usually wide awake all night freaked out. Now these shows seem totally lame, with cornball acting and obvious plots. It didn't take much to scare us or fake us out in those days. It's like when you see a play that is made for little kids. The actor comes to the front of the stage and says, "Hey kids, have you seen Bumbo the Clown? I can't find him anywhere!" And the kids are screaming at the top of their lungs, "My God man, are you blind as well as stupid? He's standing right behind you!" And the actor says "What? I can't hear you!" And the kids scream twice as loud, "Right behind you! HE'S STANDING BEHIND YOU!" The louder they yell, the more he can't hear them, by some reverse law of physics only seen at these plays. This goes on for the entire show. A word to the wise: somebody got paid for writing this script, and it could have been you.

**Sleep.** I was actually afraid of sleep. I didn't like the idea of going unconscious. Now it seems like the best part of the day. Sleep is pretty strange. If it didn't exist, and somebody made up the idea of sleep in a science fiction story, nobody would believe it. Yet we brush our teeth and go off into dreamland every night, and everybody acts like it's completely normal. That's the thing about being alive. You have to act like everything's normal.

**Dying.** The same deal as sleep, only A LOT LONGER. Yikes.

**The Basement at Night.** No way was I going down to the basement at night, except to get a soda, and that had to be done on a full run. The soda was going to fizz up, but that was better than being caught by whatever was down there.

**Spiders.** Those guys are creepy. One time I ran into a web, face-first, in the local park. That was a bad day. I never did find that spider. He is probably still on me, biding his time, chuckling the way only a spider can.

**School.** I used to throw up every year on the first day of school. It was a ritual. Rituals are important to mark the passage of time. This is what Joseph Campbell said, and he was no stranger to hurling himself. The Latin word "educare" means to "draw forth." Those Latins knew what they were talking about. Latins used to be guys from Rome, but now they are from Central America. I have no idea how that happened. I'd know the answer, but I sucked in school. I even got a "D" in water fountain.

**The Thunderbolt.** This was the big roller coaster at Willow Grove Park. It started with a steep hill that shot the coaster straight down at 70 mph, a speed that our Mercury station wagon never hit. I never went on this ride, not even in my teenage years. My little sister went on it, which was a major disgrace. This is the life of a scaredy guy.

# The Golf Ball Factory Fire

Yes, I was there at the great golf ball factory fire and explosion of 1962. I didn't start the fire, but I did see it. My brother and two sisters were there with me. We all saw it.

The day was sunny and warm. We were playing out in the yard at my grandparents' house in Rydal, PA. They lived in a big house with 9 bedrooms, 7 bathrooms, a tennis court, and huge gardens. They had great dinner parties on holidays. Like so many Americans, I have fallen a long way in life.

They had cool toys at this house, like the pedicycle in the garage. It was a three-wheeled bike from Thailand, with a passenger bench on the back. We each took turns being the native guy who did the pedaling. My grandparents bought this bike on a world tour, when they traveled around and did interesting things. That was still possible in those days.

My grandfather was a big shot with a big house. Sometimes we had to go live there for a while, when there was trouble in our house. We kind of liked it there because it made us feel rich. They had a bar with unlimited soda, a working slot machine in the basement, and a mannequin in the bathroom that scared everybody the first time they saw it.

We had trouble getting along with our grandparents. They were strict people, and they didn't tolerate any nonsense. Nonsense was our stock in trade. We were raised on nonsense, and we practiced it every day. Sometimes it was all we had. Our grandparents couldn't stand it, so there was conflict.

Also they were from the generation that said children should be seen and not heard. We couldn't say much to them, except about the weather. We were supposed to be future leaders and industrialists, so they didn't want us to mumble. We ended up shouting very loudly and clearly about the weather. It was a strain, but what could we do?

One day, we were out in the yard playing our childish games, when we noticed a plume of thick black smoke in the sky. Something was seriously burning, and it looked like it was very close to us. We started wandering towards the smoke to see what was on fire. Little kids like watching stuff burn—such as campfires, houses and factories.

We didn't tell anybody we were leaving. We kept following the smoke, and it wasn't as close we thought. We just kept walking. We weren't thinking straight, but that's what happens when you're a little kid and something new happens. You don't always think things through.

We walked for a long way, probably a couple of miles. Now there were flocks of people walking along with us, like zombies on the way to a big zombie fest, or like investors in search of that perfect deal: it's not exactly illegal, and the returns are "substantial." There was no stopping us.

We were in a crowd now, marching along toward the smoke, and there was no turning back. We didn't know where we were, or how to get back home, but it didn't worry us. Common sense wasn't our strong suit. This was something we had to see.

We followed the crowd through a big field, and then we saw it. It was a golf ball factory, and it was burning down and burning up, all at the same time. Flames hungrily licked the sky, like a kid licks an ice cream cone on a summer's day. Explosions happened every now and then, making the audience say ooh and aah like we were at a fireworks display.

We kept watching until it got dark. There were no cell phones in those days. Just when we were starting to get a little nervous, my grandmother showed up. She saw the smoke and figured that we must have wandered off to see the big event. Somehow she found us in the crowd, and gave us a ride home in her Lincoln Continental.

She always drove a Lincoln. She used to drive me to a clothing store called Robert Hall. We went there because the shirts were cheap. She had a lurching driving style, so I always felt seasick when we arrived. I didn't like the ride or the shirts, but kids didn't have choices in those days. My grandparents were trying to groom me to be a captain of industry, but I never even made lieutenant. I am barely an enlisted man.

She drove us home in the Lincoln, and gave us a good talking to. Then she made us some popcorn, and we sat down to see what was on TV. What a day.

# Schmuck with an Underwood

Some famous guy (Jack Warner) once said, "What is a writer, but a schmuck with an Underwood?" For you youngsters out there, an Underwood is brand of typewriter. A typewriter is a machine that people typed words on. Words are bunches of letters that hang around together and may or may not mean something. Jack Warner owned a movie studio. A schmuck is a writer. You'll have to take my word for it.

You have to hurry and do stuff before you die. There is a time limit here. The clock is ticking. You need to go all around the world, see the sights, pay the bills, do your job, and go to the movies. Mostly you have to stare at the computer for three hours a day, because there are messages and new cat videos waiting for you.

The computer is an incredible machine. It knows everything and can do anything, like they used to say about God, before he got into politics. You can use it to find out anything. For example, back in junior high I liked a novelty tune called "The Martian Hop." So I looked it up on the computer, and there really was such a song. Three young folks from New Jersey wrote and recorded it as a joke, and it became a big hit.

"The Martian Hop" was a great tune, and the computer remembered it well. This song was in the do-wop style, and it had an actual bass man. Novelty songs, bass men, and 45's have all left the planet and should be together now in heaven, because they were all good.

It's amazing what your computer can do. If you type the wrong word, it tells you the word that you really meant to say. How does it know? Apparently it watches you through that innocent built-in camera, and it listens in on your conversations through a little microphone that seems harmless enough. It's nothing to worry about.

So your computer knows you inside and out, and it will give you suggestions of "better" words and phrases you might use as you are typing. If you are a writer, this is a good deal. Your computer can make your book seem better than it actually is.

You can also have the computer write the entire book, thus completely skipping the middle man (you). No more struggling to come up with ideas. Most ideas have been used by now, even the ones that suck. Why strain? Mr. Computer can do it for you.

All you have to do is select "auto book" and hit the start button. You'll need to think of a catchy title, like *How to Make a Million Bucks by Using your God Given Talent to Say Things That Aren't True*, or *The Hammer and the Nail, Which One are You?* or *The Truth about Michelangelo (He was a chiseler)*.

Then you have to pick a style, like Action (violence), Romance (more violence), Spank Bottom (love), or Goth Broth (vampire cookbook). Also you need to choose a typeface for your book, like Times Roquefort, Blonde Platoon, Tater Tot Bold, Lulu Strange, Mixmaster Fred, Celestial Mint, Goofy Thing Thang, or Gluteno Free.

Then you pick some acknowledgments to put in the beginning of the book. It's time to thank somebody who inspired or irritated you. Good choices are Mom and Dad, Bill Shakespeare, or your English teacher in high school, who said you had no chance to write a book, so why doesn't he just kiss your big beige behind?

Then you have to pick a price, any price, as long as it ends in .95 (federal law). The last step is to pick a date of publication. Any day is fine; you don't need to think too much about it.

Push the button, and the book pops out. You are finished. You can lie down on the couch. Like the retired Pope, you need to take a break. When you wake up, the royalty checks will be arriving. People will want you to be on their TV shows, so you have to find a clean shirt. You must have one somewhere.

## **Money Talks**

Have you noticed that many times the majority of the citizens want something, but the opposite happens? Pick any issue. Seventy percent of the people favor a certain position, but the opposite is what they get. How is this possible?

It turns out there is a good reason for this, found in the time-honored saying, "Money talks, nobody walks." That's the secret. Money is more powerful than people. When the big money lines up on one side, the will of the people will lose every time. It won't even be close. The people don't have a chance.

Say you are a lawmaker, sitting at your desk. You hear that all the folks in your area want something. Then a gent barges into your office, whips out a checkbook, and scribbles a few figures on it. He tears out or "cuts" the check, and hands it to you. What could this mean?

It is written for a very large amount, made out to you. In the memo line it says "a little gift between friends." The date is right, and the signature looks valid. Everything is correct and proper.

"Yes, I see your point," you say. "After reading this, I have to admit, I have changed my mind. You can count on me."

"That's fine, just fine," says the gentleman. "I knew you would see it my way." Hands are shaken, and the deal is settled. This is how the system works, and why they say that money talks and nobody walks.

Clearly the man isn't going to walk home when he leaves this office. Do you think he is going to hitch a ride? Go by bicycle? Take a bus, for God's sake? He was on a bus once, when he was eleven years old. His mother made him ride the bus with her, and he never forgave her. Nobody who is anybody walks; let's put it that way.

But does money actually talk? Does it speak English? Have you ever held a dollar bill to your ear and listened? I decided to check it out for myself. The results were surprising.

The first one I tried was a single, the basic unit of America. It's good to keep a stack of them in the wallet, just for your well-being. Even if you use credit cards to buy a pack of gum, there's something comforting about that row of Georges, lined up in formation, ready to do your bidding.

According to Wikipedia, the source of all truth, single dollars are also known as bucks, bills, and bones. If you work at a fast-food place, you make eight bones an hour. It's not quite enough to stay alive, but it's close.

My house only cost 14 thousand bills, but it is in Iowa, near the railroad tracks, with a furnace that didn't work. When I was shown the house, the family was huddled around the TV, watching the movie *Poltergeist*. They were using the oven to heat the place. It was a cozy scene.

On with the experiment. I picked up one of these bucks, and held it to my ear. It was a series E bill, green, printed in 2009, personally autographed by Timothy F. Geitner. That guy must have a tired hand.

I listened carefully, and I did hear some talking. George seemed to be sad about things not turning out how he wanted, and how wallets need more ventilation.

Money is funny stuff, and it has a lot of nicknames, like: lucre, scratch, lolly, and honk. Is this where honkies got their name? Also folding stuff, dosh, milk, and scrilla. Money used to be backed by gold and silver. Now it isn't backed by anything except a very nervous guy from the government, and his bags are packed and he is edging towards the door. We trust in God but not him.

If they ever put my face on money, I would look as noble as possible, and I would use a Spanish motto "¿Por qué está aqui?" (Why are you here?) on my bill. Also I would have a picture of my house on the back, with the motto "At least it's paid for" across the top. Then a series of mysterious numbers, consisting of my locker combination from junior high plus my pants size. And then, don't forget the all-seeing eye. Like Santa, it sees you when you are sleeping or awake. No point trying to hide.

# An Audience Experience

Most people have been in an audience. It's not that hard. You have to laugh when they say something funny, listen to the music, and clap at the end. Also turn your phone off for two hours. It won't kill you.

I have been in little clubs with very small crowds. Sometimes there are more band members than audience. This is a bad scene, and a lot of pressure on the audience. What if you don't like a song that much? You have to fake a response. Ladies, you know this isn't easy.

Here's another thing that can happen when you are in an audience: the guy on stage suddenly says, "All right (name of your town here)! How are you doing tonight?"

The only possible responses are: Woo, All Right, or Yeah! What if you are feeling something else? You could try shouting:

"I am still feeling some childhood wounds!"

"I'm hungry! Can't wait to get home and make a sandwich!"

"After years of meditation practice, I no longer have a small self, so the question does not apply!"

But the guy isn't a therapist. Better stick with woo.

Some of my best memories of audience life happened at the Fillmore East auditorium in New York City. This was in the early 1970's, when I was a "student" at NYU. I had the full hippie look going, with the hair past the shoulders, and the beard growing unchecked for years, like the budget for the department of defense. My friend Rudy used to like to walk behind me at Sears, pretending he wasn't with me, so he could watch the people stare. I was freaking people out, just like young folks do now with pierces and tattoos.

*The full hippie look, NYU, 1971.*

The difference is, I could cut my hair when I felt like it. It's hard to take a tattoo off. This could be a problem later in life. I know a guy who has a swastika tattoo on his neck. That may not work so well at job interviews.

Back at NYU, when I wanted to hear some good live music, I wandered across town to the Fillmore East auditorium. One of the best acts I saw there was the legendary group, the Who.

In one memorable show, the Who were right in the middle of their set, when I heard an odd commotion in the crowd. Looking behind me, I noticed that that the lobby was on fire. Smoke was billowing into the theater in an ominous way. The regular exit was now blocked.

When you are in a theater that is on fire, it is important to head for an exit right away. It's not something you should put off until later. But this was the Who, and they were doing "Summertime Blues." I decided to stick it out and hear the rest of the tune. Not the brightest idea, but that's what I came up with.

A fire official ran down the center aisle, and jumped up on stage. Pete Townshend ran over to him and gave him a kick in the personal area, sending him flying back into the crowd, where he landed in a heap, like Uriah. The crowd gave a cheer.

Finally the song ended, and announcements were made that the building was on fire, and that the concert was over for now (boo) and any and all hippies needed to stop toking up and head for the nearest fire escape. Eventually we all made it out.

My biggest audience experience came at the original Woodstock festival. I drove up in my mother's station wagon, with some friends, some food, and Puff, the magic dragon. The car got stuck in the mud, and a farmer pulled it out with his tractor, for a hefty fee. He did so well that day that he probably bought a boat. We didn't need any concert tickets, because the area had been liberated by the People's Free Music Army.

We camped out in tents and made campfires. One guy was cutting wood with a hatchet, and he accidently sliced his own hand. He was on LSD at the time, and he said it was a cosmic experience.

No doubt we saw many great acts there. One was the Who. At one point, Abbie Hoffman rushed the stage to make some political announcements, and he received the exact same kick as the fireman. This was getting to be a routine.

Years later I saw an outdoor show in Cozumel, Mexico. A reggae band was playing a song called "Do What I Do." As the lead singer danced and moved, hundreds of folks in the audience followed along and moved in unison. We couldn't stop laughing and smiling in the crowd. That's the whole point of being in the audience, and that's what makes it all worthwhile.

# **What to Say**

Sometimes you just don't know what to say. You need the perfect remark, and you are drawing a blank. You can't think of anything that would be appropriate in the current situation.

Say you are on the phone, catching up with an old friend. You talk about the old gang, how everybody's health is going (not so hot), who is drinking or eating too much, who made a pile in real estate, who is still a bum and always will be. You go over all these topics, and more. And then it happens. You hear the toilet flush in the background. What are you supposed to say? The best choices are:

1. Gesundheit.

2. I think I'm going to be sick.

3. Good for you. Regularity is important.

4. Should I call back later, when your pants are on?

5. That reminds me, are you planning on voting this year?

6. Same to you and many more.

7. Do you live near the airport?

This is why Skype is a bad idea. Callers can see you. You have to get dressed and clean up your house before you can answer the phone. Do you want people to see your house, even if you cleaned it up? Be honest.

Speaking of honesty, Walmart is having a big promotion for a movie called *Abe Lincoln, Vampire Slayer*. This is an actual movie. Somehow this project got the green light in a Hollywood conference room. Guys and gals were gathered around a big table. A guy named Herb came in. Somebody says, "Hey Herb, what have you got?"

"You're gonna love this," says Herb, as he starts to read from a script treatment. "It's a story about Abe Lincoln as a vampire slayer. Is this a great idea, or what?"

"That's great Herb!" says Hal, trying to work up enthusiasm.

"Good job," says Mary, from the front office. "How do you come up with these?" She goes back to looking at her shoes.

Frank from the side office chimes in. "Well, it's unique!"

Everybody reaches for a doughnut, at the same time. Their hands crash at the doughnut bowl. They laugh nervously.

"Wow, I am really running late!" says Mary. "I have to pick up the kids at soccer practice," even though she doesn't have any kids and soccer practice was cancelled that day.

"Yeah, I gotta split too," says Frank, as if he were an atom or an end. "Herb, I'll catch you later."

"Cranial Sacral, look at the time! I gotta run too," says Hal, who couldn't run anywhere even if he wanted to.

They all bail out. Herb sits alone, with a plate of doughnuts. "Who am I kidding?" he says to himself. "Did I actually think that was a good idea? Have I lost my mind?"

Fast forward two years. I am looking at a poster for a movie called *Abe Lincoln, Vampire Slayer*. Back in Hollywood, Herb is driving a Studebaker XK-11 with a power pencil sharpener built right into the dash. His sunglasses cost more than I will make in my lifetime. He is on the phone with his agent, Howie.

"Yo, Howie, baby!" he is saying, even though Howie hasn't been a baby in quite a while, maybe ever. "Howie, you won't believe the idea I just came up with!"

"Lay it on me," says Howie, speaking from his swimming pool, on the inflatable raft, with the built-in TV and computer.

"Get this," says Herb. "It is called *James Madison, Quarterback*. James Madison comes back to life, and somehow gets a job as quarterback for the Green Bay Packers. That's all I have so far."

"I love it already," says Howie, as his raft capsizes, and the computer shorts out with a pop. "We can fill in the details later. You are one serious genius."

Fast forward two more years. We are in line at Walmart, looking at a poster of James Madison wearing a cheese head.

"What in the world is that?" we say to each other. (*Fade out.*)

# A Sales Pitch

Have you ever agreed to listen to a sales pitch, in order to get something free? We have done it several times, mostly on vacations. They have young folks in these vacation spots, offering to sign you up for a free gift. All you have to do to is listen while a salesman gives a talk.

Like so many things, it seems like a good idea at the time. You get free gifts or cash money, and all you have to do is sit there with a serious expression on your face, as if you are totally fascinated and intrigued by this presentation. Sound easy? Guess again, my friend.

It turns out it is about the hardest thing you ever did in your life. Just wait until you are seated at this guy's desk, with no phone calls allowed, no trips to the bathroom, and no checking your messages. Then it gets worse. The guy starts asking questions, getting your feedback, and making you interact with him. You actually have to pay attention. That's painful.

He is trying to get you to buy time shares in a condo. This condo has granite counter tops in the kitchen. You are thinking, "Who gives a flying mashed potato what the counter top is made of?" But you can't say that. You have to nod your head and say,

"Look honey, that's real granite!" And your honey has to pretend she is stoked as well. This is acting at its most difficult. Tom Hanks would have a hard time with this role.

You get a peek at your watch, and realize you have only just started. The actual presentation itself isn't even happening yet. This is just the warm-up, where the guy gets to know you better, to see what your strengths and weaknesses are, who makes the decisions, and how he can get you to sign up if enough pressure is applied.

It turns out that pressure is what makes the world go around. It's not love, desire, or mutual funds. It's pressure. These sales guys know that. They know everything, including what you are thinking right now. You are thinking you want to get the heck out of that room and onto the beach. This is mental torment, and it's how we spent many hours of precious vacation time, in search of free gifts.

One time we had a guy come right into our house to give us a sales pitch. The topic was storm windows. We were promised a hundred and fifty bucks if we would listen to his talk, pay attention, think it over, and that was it! Easy enough.

We know a woman who signed up for this talk just for the free gift, and ended up buying all new storm windows for her house. She had to take out a loan to do it. She says she is happy, but there is a haunted look in her eyes. We swore that wouldn't happen to us.

It was a good presentation, starting with a review of our current windows, which I have to admit are mostly "total pieces of crap" as they say in the window industry. Some of them leak air, and some are painted shut. Our windows are junk.

His windows, on the other hand, are the stuff that dreams are made of. They go up and down with the touch of a finger. We agreed that we would like them in our house, if the price was right. We should never have admitted that.

The price kept coming down, like the glass ball on New Year's Eve. Somehow the guy's supervisor got into the act, all the way from Arkansas. I had to get on the phone and talk to him. He said things were going great in Arkansas, which I was glad to hear. I told him things were also pretty good in Iowa.

The price came down one more time. Carol went over to the computer and feigned typing an e-mail. I poured myself an iced tea, and tried to look casual. Carol started to weaken. Maybe we should do it, she whispered, when she had a chance. Our defense system was crumbling around us. We would have left the premises, but he would have gone with us.

Finally he lowered the price so low that he must have lost his own personal mind. Still no sale. Now the truth was out. We weren't really going to buy those windows. We were moochers, only in it for the free gift. Disgusted, the guy packed up his stuff and slid out the door. We breathed a sigh of relief.

Was it worth it? Yes, says Carol. We got the gift. I am not so sure. We paid the price. Now we have that haunted look.

## Snowflakes Are Our Friends

I was at somebody's house watching TV. By watching TV, I mean we were going through the channels one at a time, spending about half a second on each. You get a good idea what the show is like in half a second. If you don't see any explosions or cars flying in the air, you move on.

We stopped for a few seconds on one channel. An airplane was landing in a snowstorm, and the snowflakes looked familiar. "Wait a minute," I said. "I think this might be *Die Hard*."

After a while my friend realized I was right. "How did you know?" he said.

"I recognized one of the snowflakes in the beginning," I said. He was impressed.

So the thing they tell you in school about snowflakes is true. No two are the same. They are individuals, just like you and me. Each one has its own style, personality, and dumb political beliefs. Any snowflake could be president someday, as long as it can raise five billion dollars, and it doesn't melt during the primaries.

In the old days, snow was a big part of life, especially when snowstorms caused school closings. What a gift from God. You had a big report due the next day, and it required gobs of preparation and research, none of which had happened due to personal reasons which trained psychologists couldn't figure out. There was trouble ahead, a disaster rolling up like a slow freight train and no way to stop it. And then these little innocent white flakes start to fall, and they keep falling, and you are cheering them on, go flakes, go! Then the next morning, the TV man reads your school name, right after Be-bop Christian and before Tenderloin Tech. He confirms that school is closed. It is a miracle that came from the sky, so praise and thanks are in order, along with sledding.

In those days they used to block off certain streets in our township, such as Walt Lane, just so the kids could go sledding. I don't know what happened to the people who lived there. Hopefully they had provisions to keep themselves alive until the spring thaw. Or maybe they were sacrificed so we could sled.

The cool kids had Flexible Flyer sleds, and they probably drive Jaguars now. We had crappy sleds from Sears, but they did the job. Sometimes kids would "ditch" us on the way down the hill, so we would skid off the road and get a face full of snow. I did get to see a lot of snow, up close and personal.

And now up to present day life in Iowa. We are in the middle of the Winter from Heck. The temperature plunged like a lady's neckline at the Academy Awards, and it has stayed there for longer than anybody can stand. This winter just won't quit.

Why do they even have such cold weather? Nobody likes it. We never voted on it, that I can remember, but I might have missed an announcement. Everybody is bundled up and miserable, plus sniffling. We can't go outside for more than a few minutes without freezing to death. What sort of way is this to live?

My sister moved to Hawaii. She can swim in the ocean every day. She wears shorts, and she is not shivering. When I talk to her on the phone she tries to act like she is cold, just to make me feel better, but she isn't fooling anybody. She is sane, and clearly the rest of us have lost our minds.

*My sister's front yard in Hawaii. This is the sane life.*

I did watch some of the Winter Olympics the last few nights. There is a big TV where I "work." I put the word "work" in quotes because we shouldn't kid ourselves. This job consists of walking up and down the halls making sure the building is not on fire. I'm not kidding you.

A lady was watching the Olympics so I sat down and joined her. We saw a little bit of curling, which is a satire on a sport. It is Olympic sweeping. Do housekeepers enjoy watching it?

We also saw the speed skating and trick skiing, which are both exciting. They are modernizing the games and putting in crazy stuff that the kids made up, like flipping upside down while wearing skis, doing two revolutions in the air, checking your e-mails, then landing backwards and skiing the rest of the way down the slope on your head. The judges will give a high score for that one.

## Being Sick, It's a Part of Life

Life has a lot of parts. Sometimes good things happen, like chocolate cake, a ten dollar bill that blows under your shoe with nobody chasing it, and old Charlie Chan movies on the Internet. Don't forget sunsets, puppies, and all the things on calendars. There is so much beauty and happiness in our world!

But we have to admit there are bad parts of life too, like Melba toast, nuclear war, and being sick. Sometimes you get sick, and you have to be miserable for a while. Then to your great relief it latches onto your best friend, and now he has to deal with it.

There was a bad sickness this year that went around town. Everybody got it, including me. I had the dreaded "cough that won't go away." It seemed like it would never end, like a ride to Denver on the Trailways bus. Coughing has to be one of the least fun things that a person can spend their time doing. There aren't many people who cough for the fun of it.

Who invented coughing? I hate to say this, but I think it might have been God. I wish I had the copyright on coughing. Then every time somebody coughed, they'd owe me a nickel. If there was a flu outbreak, it would be great news for me. This is why guys who run drug companies and hospitals are always in such a good mood.

How did I get sick, anyway? I remember it like it was yesterday. A stray germ landed on my hand at the water fountain. He looked kind of lonely and tense. I felt sorry for him. His name was Germy. He climbed onto my fingertip and hung on for all he was worth. He was a tough little guy, and he was pretty strong for his size.

Later I rubbed my chin. Germy saw his big chance. He jumped with all his might, and landed on my face. Then he set up camp and waited. The next day, he did nothing but rest and lie low. The day after that he wrote some letters home, and checked out his equipment. The following day, he was ready to break camp and begin the long climb up Nostril Alley. It took him a full day to make the climb. He was almost killed by a random sneeze, but he hung on. He's tough.

Eventually he made it into the bloodstream, where apparently he had a lot of romantic encounters. I don't want to know the details, I didn't ask, it's none of my business; but soon he had a lot of kids, grandkids, cousins, and in-laws. Imagine keeping track of all those birthdays and weddings, and buying presents for everybody. What do you get for a young germ and his wife who are just starting out and really need everything?

Now my body is filled with germs. I am sneezing them out every day. It got so bad that the doctor was involved. She didn't come to my house. Those days are over, my friend. They went out with the hula hoop and the Desoto roadster. What a car that was, and what a fad.

I can actually remember the doctor pulling up to our house in his big Cadillac, back in the old days. He had a black bag, full of dreaded needles and medicine. We hated him because he gave us shots that made our arms hurt. He lived next to my grandparents, and he raised pigeons, which by coincidence carry disease. Makes you wonder.

The good part about being sick was a kid could stay home from school and watch *I Love Lucy* on TV, instead of sitting in a classroom hearing about the Vikings and their invasions. They wiped out a lot of people, and we honor and admire them. World history turns out to be a series of mass murderers, from Genghis to Adolf. A hundred years from now, kids will be studying Jeffrey Dahmer in school. They'll have to memorize the layout of his apartment for a quiz on Friday.

Apparently we are down here on this planet to learn lessons. Meanwhile, some celestial beings with giant books, big quill pens and unlimited ink are keeping track of how we are doing. It would be cool if they gave us magic powers on earth, like the power to speak Italian, or the power to make certain political parties dissolve overnight with a slight fizzing sound.

But they don't give us these exotic powers, so we have to make it on our own. Meanwhile, Germy is holding a family reunion in my head. I hate that guy.

# **An Experiment in Terror**

Tonight I decided to try an experiment. Instead of the usual semi-healthy dinner, I will eat a whole bag of potato chips. What will happen? How will I feel? What will be the consequences? Will I survive? I decide to keep a scientific diary to measure the results.

**Preamble:** *Potato chips formed a major part of my diet while growing up; along with soda (you need something to wash them down). We had a big tin can of Charles Chips underneath the TV table. That's a good location, because they go well with TV. I also had them for lunch every day in Thomas Williams Junior High. At fancy dinner parties, potato chips were the appetizer. Chips were a big deal to me.*

**7:15 PM**—What a selection in the store. At least 25 yards of potato chips down one aisle. I went with a bag of Country Faire rippled chips, for two reasons: 1) They are cheap, and 2) That's about it. I always check the ingredients, just for a laugh. Nothing in there but potatoes, oil, and salt. There seems to be some confusion about what particular oil was used. Was it cottonseed, peanut, or motor oil? Apparently they forgot. They went back and asked the cook, and he drew a total blank. "Never happened to me before," he says. "I made that batch two or three days ago. All I can tell you is, I just don't know." They try hypnosis, regression therapy, bribes, and threats. He still can't remember, so they have to list all the different oils they keep around the shop. It has to be one of them.

**7:20**—Got in the line. A newspaper headline says that Rona and Rodney are getting a divorce. Their marriage is a shambles. Cheating may have been involved. Well, I'll be darned. Lawyers have been called in. These people must be famous, but who are they? Plus diet tips. They are guaranteeing 20 pounds off in 20 days, but they don't know about the potato chips.

**7:25**—I have paid, and I am out in the parking lot. I broke right into the chips, even before starting the car. It was a moment of passion. On the way home the radio was playing "Lay Down Sally" by Eric Clapton. That has got to be some of the best driving home music ever recorded. I wheeled out of the parking lot just as the guitar solo was starting.

**7:28**—I'm already home. That's the good part about living in a small town.

**7:30**—I pop a movie into the computer and get out some onion dip. If onion dip is involved, you know tomorrow is going to be a bad day. I'm going to wake up with toxic waste taste, like a French poodle did a petite number deux in my mouth. Can't worry about it now.

**7:55**—The movie is only fair, but I decide to stick it out. Like men, good movies are hard to find. Plowing steadily through the chips.

8:45—The movie ended. The young couple was holding hands, but did they really love each other? We have serious doubts about these two. Everybody is hiding something, but that's the nature of being alive. I don't feel so hot.

9:00—Feeling down, not worthy, unhappy. Need to escape. Must get away.

9:10—I think the potato chips have clogged my brain. My hypothalamus is shivering, my liver has smoke coming out the back, and my chakras decided to take the day off. All systems are in panic mode.

9:15—My digestive system is not really a system anymore. It's a disaster area. There are fire trucks and national guardsmen on the scene. Reporters are demanding to know what happened and why, but I am not answering the door.

9:45—Now I'm getting philosophical. There was a guy who died today in our town. Energetic guy, leading an active life, fitness buff. Suddenly he heard Gabriel blowing his horn, so he stopped what he was doing and said "here I come." He fell down and rose up, and he was gone. It made me feel weird, so I bought some potato chips. I tried to call it a celebration, but didn't fool anybody. It was just one of those nights.

9:50—The recovery process starts. Apologies all the way around, and a big pot of tea is brewing. I won't do this again for a while. Starting first thing tomorrow, I will be a better person.

## **Shooting Stars**

The other day I went with Carol to Iowa City, just to be somewhere different. We have to get out of town every now and then, or we'll go nuts. There are already enough people going nuts. We don't want to add to the pile.

We got lost at one point, and tried to ask pedestrians for directions, but we couldn't get anybody's attention. They were all wearing headphones. If we texted them they would have replied, but they aren't into the "real world" so much. I don't blame them.

We went to the movie theater to see what was playing, but the films didn't look great. One was about a guy who attacked people with a chain saw. That was his hobby and his creative outlet. We decided to skip the movies. Carol shopped, and I wandered around the mall.

I saw a security cop doing his rounds. I am kind of elderly myself, but he looked like he could have been my dad. He was carrying a firearm in a holster, but if the shooting were to start, I don't think he would become the guy from *The Matrix*, doing backflips in slow motion while picking guys off one at a time. I'm not even sure they gave him any ammo.

I shot a gun one time in my life. That was at Admiral Farragut Academy Summer Camp. I was in a platoon of little kids who marched around in military formation. We could even do the difficult *Double to the rear harch*, which you would have to see to believe. We were mostly going to ball games, plus swimming in the mighty (dirty) Toms River. We also went to the rifle range.

Yes, they gave us real guns to shoot. We shot in the prone position, which means lying down. To our disappointment we didn't learn how to "draw" like in the old Westerns.

They gave us a rifle called the 22, which is slightly bigger than the 21. We were aiming at little targets made of paper. We could only point the gun in one direction, towards the target. The rest of us were safely behind the action.

One kid turned around with a loaded gun in his hands, and for a second he was pointing it in our direction. He enjoyed watching us scream and dive for cover. That made his day, and probably his whole summer. Luckily no shots were fired.

That is my whole experience using a gun in this incarnation on Earth. We didn't have any firearms around the house when I was growing up. My grandfather had some pistols locked up in his house, and a little target range outside, where the laundry was hung. That laundry deserved to be hung. It was guilty and got what was coming to it.

My grandmother used to shoot skeet at her country club. She yelled "pull" and a guy launched a clay pigeon into the air. She blasted it to smithereens with a shotgun. Later she played golf and had some lunch. It was a strict routine.

The only time I ever saw a gun being pointed at somebody in real life was in the 1970's. I was renting a place with a guy, and we were in a rock band together. We got to be pretty good, but pretty good doesn't count when you are a musician. If you aren't Bruce Springsteen, then you are performing in bars at 2 in the morning. Later you are loading amps into an old van. After a couple of years of that, a real job starts to look good.

There was a little "head shop" next to our house. This is a place run by longhairs, selling products made by longhairs, to promote the longhair way of life. If you smoked pot, and you liked beads and posters, this was the place for you.

One day somebody took something without paying for it. The owner ran out into the street, pointed a pistol in the guy's face, and demanded his merchandise. He didn't say whether the gun was loaded or not, but he was holding it with two hands, just like they do on TV. The days of peace and love were over. Some heavy karma was going down if his property didn't come back.

It does get your attention when a guy is waving a gun around and hollering. You stop what you are doing and watch carefully. You don't make any sudden moves. For example, you wouldn't fling a Frisbee at the guy. As far as I know, nobody was shot. That place closed down, the 70's ended, and everybody got haircuts. That's all I can tell you.

## What Happened to Potter?

Potter was my father. That was his middle name, and that's what we called him when we were growing up. It was always Potter, not dad, pop, or father. He was a quiet guy, a gentle soul, living as best he could in our family whirlwind.

When Potter was a little kid, he got sick. He was in bed for a year, and it wasn't certain that he would survive. He did, but after that he was kind of a spaced out guy. He was also blind in one eye. He wasn't the sharpest fellow.

He went into the army during World War II. He was with the 398th Bombardment group, stationed in England. He was a radio mechanic, but who knows how he managed that, since he wasn't mechanical and didn't know anything about radios. I guess when a war happens you do whatever they tell you to do.

Since Potter was a little spaced out, he had trouble remembering his left from his right while marching around. They made him paint a big "*L*" and "*R*" on his shoes with white paint, so he would turn the right way. This is the only thing I know about his war service. He never talked about it. None of the ex-soldiers did. I think they all wanted to forget about it, and besides, "we can't handle the truth." A lot of them hit the bottle pretty hard.

After the war, Potter married my mother. They bought a house, and started a family with four kids, a big turtle, and an assortment of dogs. It was the baby boom, and it was pretty loud in our house, that's for sure. My mother was in charge of decision making and discipline. Potter tried to stay low and go with the flow. What ever happened was pretty much OK with him.

Potter never expressed strong opinions about anything. I don't know what he felt about politics, civil rights, or the Taft Hartley Act. I don't even know if he liked the mountains or the shore for a vacation spot. He just got in the car and went along with the rest of us when it was time to go. My mother made the calls and he followed instructions like the rest of us.

*Our father, who leadeth us to the shore.*

I know he liked the Civil War. He read books about it. He also liked to smoke Parliaments, have a beer after work, and play bridge. This is what people did in those days.

Potter was a really sweet guy. We liked to climb up on him when he got home from work. Every day he rode the train into town to the Philco Company, which is where guys from Philly worked. They didn't say what they did there, and we didn't ask.

Potter cut the grass on the weekend with the old Gravely tractor. Gravely, he cut the grass. He also raked leaves, and tended to our ancient coal furnace. In the fall he hung up heavy wooden storm windows around the house.

One year I got a special birthday gift. I got to go with Potter to New York City for the weekend. It was just the two of us, a father and son deal. We rode up on the train, and stayed in a big hotel. We never went hunting, fishing, camping, or any rough stuff like that. We were from the suburbs.

Just when he was settled in a middle-age groove, Potter's job came to a sudden end. His company was taken over by Ford Motors. Many workers were let go, laid off, jettisoned, and downsized. Potter was one of them, and he had to come up with a new career.

He got a job as a real estate salesman. He ended up being good at it. He had a laid-back, no-pressure approach that people liked and could trust. He did well.

One night we got a phone call. Somebody said there was something wrong with Potter. My mother ran out of the house and drove away to see him. She came home a couple of hours later, and said Potter had died. His heart had given out.

We were stunned. He was only 50 years old. I was only in junior high. We were little kids. Our father wasn't supposed to be dead yet. We were all in shock. They had a big service and the school principal came, and so did our friends. We didn't know what to say or do.

We all just kept going. My brother and I learned how to tend the coal furnace. If the fire went out at night, my mother would yell for us to "wake up and re-start the damn furnace." That's the worst yell you can ever hear. We had to get out of bed, put on old clothes, shovel coal, and light the furnace. The old days weren't always so great.

# The Magic Tube

TV was a big part of our lives when I was "growing up." I put that last phrase in quotes, because it may not have actually happened. I did get taller over the years, and then wider. The widening process is still underway. Actual maturity may have been missed along the way.

We were the first generation to grow up watching TV. The result? We are dumb as rocks. They have elections every four years to prove it. The candidates like to brag about how stupid they are. "My opponent calls himself dumb," says one guy. "Don't make me laugh. I'm way stupider than he is." He isn't kidding either.

The TV was always on in our house. Sometimes I would wake up on a Saturday morning at the crack of noon, and I would hear conversations coming from the kitchen. People were yukking it up and having a good old time. I would hustle downstairs to join the gang. When I got there, I realized it was just the TV that was making all the noise. That's the beauty of TV: it makes life seem like more fun than it actually is.

On school days, the TV was on while we were getting ready for another day of scholastic failure and humiliation. In Philly there was a guy named Wee Willie Weber who told jokes and also predicted the weather, sometimes both at once. We ate our Pop-Tarts, drank our Tang, and went off into the unknown.

At dinner we had to draw numbers to see who would get to be closest to the TV. Many characters came into our house, such as Harriet and Ozzie. This is the Ozzie with the sweater, not the guy who bit the heads off bats. Also Lassie was there barking away, and the people had to figure out what she meant. When our dogs barked we yelled at them to shut up.

There were also many special events on TV that we all sat around and watched:

**The Indianapolis 500.** I don't know if they were laps or miles, but we watched them all, including the pit stops. Those guys can really change a tire in a hurry. In those days, anybody could watch a car race on TV. You didn't have to be a Republican.

**The Miss America Pageant.** I think they should skip the talent and speeches, and go back to having a simple beauty contest. If you were watching a muscleman contest, would you want one of the guys to come out of his pose and explain his feelings about world peace? It wouldn't be natural.

**The Wizard of Oz.** Flying monkeys, melting witches, and the Lullaby League of Women Voters. This movie had it all.

**Moon Landings.** People actually landed on the moon, shot a round of golf, and flew back home in time for the holidays. Were those early landings faked, or have people gotten stupider?

**The Original Titanic.** How many times did we see that big boat go down? The captain had a nice beard. I'll say that for him.

**King Kong.** The most exciting movie ever made. It wasn't until years later that I realized it was actually a show about slavery in America. Did everybody know this but me?

**The Beverly Hillbillies.** Not much can be said here.

**Serious Sad Events.** Every now and then they interrupted our programming for a special announcement: yet another famous person had been shot. At first it was a stunning shock. Then it got to be a fad. Weird stuff becomes normal if you watch it enough times on TV.

*The author "standing by" the family TV, late 1950's.*

In the later stages of childhood I got to have my own personal TV in my bedroom, thanks to the Green Stamps that my mother collected from our local Acme food store. I guess she figured I was already living in a dream world, so I might as well have entertainment. I watched the late movie every night and had to stay up to see how it came out, so I wasn't the sharpest tack in the box the next day in school. I only had a vague idea of what the teachers were talking about. For example, I thought the potatoes went hungry during the potato famine.

Many experts tried to figure out how many hours we had spent in our lives watching TV, how many murders we had seen, and how many commercials we had observed while growing up. They finally threw up their hands and said it was more than they could count. Basically, it was our whole lives.

We watched TV instead of actually doing stuff, which was a whole new way to be a person. Now everybody does it. You can sit in a chair and stare in one direction for hours on end without doing or saying anything. You see people in their houses at night, in a daze, with the TV flickering like a strobe light or a campfire. All you know is, they are having an experience.

## What the Guys are Saying

I know one guy in town who says he is going to have his house painted. He bought a new house for himself, and he wants to have the interior painted "just so." You know how it is when you are moving into a new place. You want everything to look nice and neat.

I asked him who was doing the painting and he said it was a guy named Jesús , but he couldn't remember the last name.

"Was it Christ?" I asked him, coming up with the first name I could think of. "With long hair and a beard? Nice smile?"

He said no, I must be thinking of someone else. That guy was a carpenter, but he didn't do house painting. And we wish our friend well with his new house.

Another guy has been telling me about chemtrails. These are lines in the sky made either by innocent jet plane exhaust, or by evil government scientists, depending on who you believe. He is sure it is the second one. It has something to do with controlling the weather and trying to kill us all, because that is what the government does.

I get mad at the government sometimes, like when one of their agents fires up his blinking lights and pulls me over for a speeding ticket. I have said many bad words in very naughty combinations when that has happened. But I don't think the officer goes home, eats a chicken sandwich, and then climbs into his black helicopter and goes into the sky to create lines that poison our air supply. "Anything is possible," is the old saying, but like most sayings it sounds good but isn't true.

Another guy was telling me about the Iraqi Dinar. This is an investment that he heard about. This is actual money from Iraq that you can use to buy sodas and cars if you live over there. Somehow these dinars got devalued to the point where you can buy thousands of them at a time with pocket change. Some "experts" are saying that a twenty dollar investment in dinars could make you thousands of dollars down the line.

This guy himself is an Iraqi millionaire. He showed me a million dollar bill that he bought on line. If the money goes up as far as people think, he will be richer than the Donalds Trump and Duck combined. I hope if it happens he takes us all out to "dinar."

Yet another guy was telling me about a home in a nearby town that had a lot of house pets in it. The police heard about it and had a look. They were shocked. So far they have counted over 300 live animals in there. These were all types of animals: including sheep, turkeys, rats, sugar gliders (don't ask), mice, and skunks. He had a couple of dogs and cats as well.

There were also 56 hissing cockroaches found in special cages. These are roaches that "hiss when you pat them," according to the newspaper. I swear I am not making this up. Being a landlord, I have seen my share of roaches. I have seen some that giggle when you pat them. Some purr and flip over on their backs, hoping for a tummy rub. Others do the Charleston. But I have never heard of a cockroach that hisses when you pat it. This is a hard one to understand.

That's a lot of animals to have in your house. When I was growing up we had three dogs at the same time. If somebody set them off they made a barking explosion. If you were an intruder trying to break into our house (God knows why you would want to: nothing in there was worth much, and the doors were wide open anyway) you would turn right around and go the other way.

For a while we had six or seven cats in our house in Iowa at the same time. It was an approximate number because some were part time. They stopped by our house for a bite to eat every now and then, just to see what we were serving. Everywhere you looked you saw another animal. It was about the limit a sane person could handle.

That's why you have to wonder about having 300 animals, including farm animals, living with you in your pad. This is extreme. Either this guy really liked animals, or else, what?

# **Hash Songs**

Years ago people were predicting we would become a totally cashless society. I never thought it would happen, but it has. Everybody is broke. We made it.

There is a new James Bond film at the theaters. Hard to believe they are still going. I remember seeing *Goldfinger* when I was a youngster, with my friends. What a theme song! We had no idea that one human could do so many cool things. Rockets that fired out of his car—why didn't we think of that? We made some crude attempts to rig up projectiles that flew off our cars and caused mischief. This was the ultimate in suave living.

Watching James Bond is part of growing up. This is where we learned how to handle dice, cards, ladies, and martinis—everything you really need to know, that as usual they don't teach you in school. Plus James had a special license to kill anyone he felt needed it. How do you get one of those?

Another part of being a little kid is singing naughty songs. These songs have many bad words in them. There was one about Canal Street in New Orleans. The hero of the song went walking down Canal Street, knocking on every door, trying to find a lady to go out on date with him, without much luck. This made him say a whole string of bad words in a row. He finally does hook up with a young lady, but they have problems with their relationship. Let's put it that way. This causes yet another string of bad words. Then he has to go the doctor and get some medicine, and here come the bad words, one more time.

Any kid listening to this is laughing so hard that is rolling on the ground with stuff coming out of his nose. This delightful song was passed on from one youth to the next, in the underground dirty song network. Parents, TV, radio, all the media, are totally out of the picture on this one.

Then there was the saga of William, the barnacled sailor. There are many verses to this song, each one telling the story of love. Boy goes on shore leave, meets girl, and later makes up ribald song. It's very romantic.

There was a song about a guy who was looking over his dead dog Rover, that he overlooked before. Another one had a holiday theme. It is about the three kings from the Orient who are trying to smoke a rubber cigar. Once again, hard to top this for entertainment value.

Who wrote these songs? Did they make any money from them, or did they die paupers working for Jim's Tire and Repair out on the highway? The moral of the story: if you write a ribald song about a sailor and his girlfriend, COPYRIGHT IT.

I looked this up on the Internet, and it turns out there is a name for these tunes. They are called hash songs. This is an actual musical genre, like pops or weasel. There are websites devoted to these songs. Some are original tunes, and some are parodies of famous songs. Hash songs are offensive, immature, sexist, and blasphemous. Some of them got their start as rugby songs and beer-drinking songs.

We should have known beer was involved. Beer, along with coffee and gasoline, make up the "big three" liquids that Americans love to consume. That's what makes this country great.

There are whole collections, or hymnals, of these songs, and some of them have been recorded. They even have websites that print out the lyrics. One website is run by an outfit named Flying Booger.

I decided to call on the executives of Flying Booger, to see if I could interview them and write their history. I went to their corporate offices, in Westchester, New York. Nice landscaping, scenic ponds, pretty good fountain. There is a guard booth at the entrance to block me from going any further. I didn't have an appointment, so the guy turned me away. It isn't easy doing journalism. Don't kid yourself.

## We Need the Funnies

It's a tough world out there. I know a lady who was arrested for eating a donut. She picked it up on the way through the supermarket, and polished it off before she got to the checkout line. She thought no one would know the difference. Well, the police were waiting for her when she got out the door. Now this will be on her record (she is putting out an album of greatest hits). Plus it will be written up in the police blotter in next week's paper. Luckily nobody gets the paper anymore, so not that many people will know about it.

I just saw a picture of the old *Philadelphia Inquirer* newsroom. It was empty, because they cut way back on staff. I grew up reading that paper. OK, I didn't actually read it, but I did check out the comic page to look at Beetle Bailey. That guy always seemed to be in trouble. He reminds us a lot of ourselves. That's the beauty of comic strips.

They also had serious comics, which seems like a paradox, but there you have it. They had Dr. Jim Thornburg, M.D. This strip deals with important issues that are faced by the good doctor as he goes about his daily routine. For example, one patient might have a sore throat. This story could go on for months. You check half a year later, and they are still on the same topic. So how's the throat, Dr. T asks the patient, Miss Mulberry. She says it is still bothering her. Stay tuned for more developments.

They also had a bridge column, which I used to like to read, but I am not sure why, not being a bridge player or even understanding the rules. It was written by a nice fellow who used to be a famous movie actor. I liked that he called people "North" or "South" instead of their names. This would be handy at parties, when you can't remember somebody's name. You could just say Yo East, how's it going? Also there was another guy who wasn't too bright that he called the Dummy. You could use that one at parties too.

This newspaper also had the *New York Times* crossword puzzle but it was usually way beyond me. By the end of the week, I couldn't even understand the clues. Here's one for 17 across: "Bartholomew's Muse, more or less." Apparently there are people who can solve these puzzles.

The advice lady was fun to read. Somebody wants to know who to marry—the nice guy with the muscles, or the jerk with the Ferrari. She says go with the jerk. The muscles will fade away, but you can always sell the Ferrari.

Back in elementary school, the time of terror, we studied newspapers. We also had our own paper called *The Young Citizen* given to us every week, so we could practice reading it. It's not as easy as it looks. Guys on the bus can fold it with a snap of the wrist, but that takes practice.

This paper covered all the big stories of the day, but it left out the most important part—the funnies. They wanted us to be serious citizens who made informed decisions. They tried their best, but it didn't work.

We also had to write our own editorials. Most of the kids took serious topics, like the latest transit strike in Philly. Was it a bad thing or a terrible thing? And what about the Russians—should we hate them or despise them? I wrote mine about the funny papers, called "The Funnies are Important."

I argued that the funnies really are important. They make people feel better. They give us a little lift, as we are riding the train into town to some horrible job. If these little kids, dogs, and cavemen could bring a smile to our faces, that was a good thing. They had a purpose.

We also took a class trip to see the Inquirer Building. The most impressive part of the tour was the basement, because there were railroad cars in there. They backed the cars right into the building and loaded the latest edition of the paper into the train. That's about as cool as it gets.

Later I drove a school bus in Philly, and took a busload of kids on a field trip to the Inquirer Building. But the teacher didn't know he had to make a reservation. You can't just show up in the editorial room with a busload of screaming kids. We were turned away. I drove them to a video arcade, and dropped the kids off there. They ran inside in a mob. The teacher said they could catch a bus home. This really happened. I hope they all made it home OK.

## Two Screenplays

I'm working on a new screenplay called *Nice Try Kids*. It's about a baseball team made up of happy, well-adjusted high school students. These are some of the most popular, successful, and self-confident kids in the whole school. Everybody likes them.

They are also excellent athletes. They have a "no drop" policy, where any ball that is hit in the air is caught, no matter how hard the catch might be. Double and even triple plays are routine for them. One time they could have had a quadruple play, but they figured there wasn't any point.

As the season goes along, everything goes downhill. The kids start getting into trouble with the law, and into substance abuse. They become more antisocial. Their coach, who is a wonderful guy, runs into trouble with his marriage, and he starts to hit the bottle. Finally he is admitted to the hospital.

The kids come to see him and ask if they should win the big game for him. "What do I care?" he says, and then goes into a big coughing attack.

The kids start acting out at home and on the field. Nobody likes them anymore. They are now a ragtag gang of loners and misfits. They have lost all confidence. They just don't see the point in trying anything.

Finally they are in the last game of the season. They are favored to win, but they blow the game. Easy pop flies drop right between three players. They run the bases backwards. They lose, 35 to nothing. On the way home, the team bus crashes through a barricade.

Critics can start criticizing a movie in advance, before it even comes out. (Nobody knows how they do it.) Already they have a lot to say about this film, with plenty of exclamation points:

"A must-not see!!"

"Two thumbs way down, and all fingers and toes as well!"

"The feel-bad movie of the year!"

"This film will make you cry, but not in a good way!"

*Nice Try Kids* is the name of the project. Like a muscle group on a guy who goes to the gym, it is in development. Investors are welcome. Prospectus provided upon request.

The other project is a murder mystery, called *The Case of the Negligent Negligee*. Everyone is a suspect. You don't know who did it. It could be anyone, except the person you think did it.

The butler has been busy. He took the fireplace poker, wiped the blood off it and buried it in the back yard, his features grimly lit by lightning flashes. Nothing suspicious there.

Then he went into the garage, and wiped the blood off of the car's fenders. (They really don't pay him enough.) Then he wiped the blood off the front door and welcome mat. You just can't find help like this anymore.

Lady Chapman spent the day trying to wipe the blood off her pocketbook. She claimed it got there "by an unknown person she met in the locker room." Her story checked out, except the part about the locker room, the pocketbook, and the blood.

Meanwhile, Miss Pringle was trying to wash the blood off her towels, without much luck. She tried everything, including both New and Old Tides. She says she "forgot" how it got there. Why would she lie? For that matter, why would she tell the truth?

Colonel Bodger had a dickens of a time getting the blood off his golf clubs. He had to stash them next to the chesterfield, because there was a body behind the whatnot. Plausible enough.

Then the power went out. Somebody screamed. When the lights came back on, somebody screamed again. They tested the lights. Every time they went off there was a scream and another when they went back on. They'd have to bring the electrician in again.

Kathy Kline, girl detective, had her hands full with this case. Just then, she noticed a fiber on the carpet. She looked at it with her detective microscope. Sure enough, it was a carpet fiber. This was going to be a tough case.

# High School Sweethearts

You never forget your high school sweetheart, no matter how long you live. You'll be sitting there, ninety years old, saying "That sweetheart was really something." And then you let out a big sigh. At least we hope it was a sigh.

I was talking recently to my friend Rob. He was reminiscing about a girl he knew in high school, over 40 years ago. He still remembers the little miniskirts she wore, just like it was yesterday. She walked into English class and sat down at her desk, and her miniskirt would rise up. It is such a precious memory to him. Then he let out a big sigh. He will never forget her as long as he lives.

I know several people who recently reunited with their high school sweethearts. These are older folks, in their 50's and 60's. Some of them are retired. Somehow they got back with their old flames from the twelfth grade. These are their stories.

Jack went to his high school reunion in his old hometown. He met up with a lady he used to know. In those days she was just a kid in junior high and he thought she was a little pest. They started talking, and the age difference wasn't so big anymore. The next thing you know, they got married.

Jack was into meditation and Eastern philosophy. She considered all that to be the work of the devil. You don't have to be psychic to see trouble ahead.

Jack said one night he took his dinner plate, and threw it across the room like a Frisbee. He was surprised how well it flew. It traveled a surprising distance, on an even keel, and the payload of dinner stayed mostly onboard for the flight. The plate was full of spaghetti at the time. If you could have framed the area where it crashed, you could have called it art. The marriage didn't last.

Another friend named Joe was sitting around his house one day, when who should show up at the door but his high school girl friend. She had split with her husband, and was there to announce that she was single once again. They mingled, and then got married.

It was great for a while. They had a nice house with a working lava lamp and a dog that didn't do much except bark. He barked at anything that moved, and even things that didn't move, like trees. They seemed like a solid couple, until Joe decided to have a fling with a lifeguard at the pool. That sank their relationship again, like the *Pequod* going down for a second time.

And then there was the story of Jim. He was sitting there at the computer one day minding his own business, when a facebook message came in. It was from his old high school sweetie. Somehow by a miracle she found him on line. She still remembered him after all these years.

Of course she did. They were really serious back in high school. Jim wanted to marry her then, but he didn't have an actual job or any means of support. They figured they would get by somehow. Her father heard about the plan, and had a little talk with Jim.

"Jim," he said, "you're a good kid. I like you. But I have to tell you something. My daughter is going to college. She is not going to marry you. In fact, if you don't leave town, I'll kill you. That's a fact. I'm not trying to threaten you or make you nervous. I say this as a friend."

She was a great gal, but not worth getting killed over, so he left town. She started a new life, with a series of marriages, kids, and cats. Jim connected with her on line, so many years later. He flew to California to see her, and never came back. Pretty soon they were married.

So how did it work out? Like a fairy tale. They are living happily ever after. They walk on the beach every day. They are having the time of their lives.

I also know two couples—call them the *Ishmaels* and the *Rockets*—who got together in high school, got married, and stayed together all their lives. They are still going strong, even now. Nobody knows how they did it.

So, this is the power of high school sweethearts. No matter how many years go by, you always remember them. (Sigh.)

# **What did Betty Do?**

Betty was my mother. The question is, what did Betty do?

1. She insisted on being called Betty. She didn't want to be known as ma, mom, mother, mater, or jet. I was embarrassed when people heard me call her Betty.

2. She ran an open household. Friends and strangers could walk right into the house at any time. On Friday nights there might be 10 kids sleeping over. The dogs could also come and go as they pleased. They travelled and crapped at will. All the dogs were loose back then, and so were the kids.

3. She brought me down to see the trains at the Philadelphia train station. I could sit there for hours and watch trains come and go. I was easily amused.

4. People had a hard time understanding her when she spoke, because she had a cleft palate. Sometimes she got frustrated to the point of tears on the phone.

*Betty with baby Linda. You can feel the love.*

5. She ran her own indexing company, right out of her bedroom, on a big old wooden desk. She created indexes for medical books. This was before computers, so she put the entries in alphabetical order by hand. We kids used to help sometimes, so we got pretty good with the alphabet.

6. She tried to help me come out of my shell, and do well in life, but it was hopeless. All the experts said I was a "late bloomer." Fifty years later, we are still waiting.

7. She cooked dinners. It's hard to believe now, but the whole family sat down and ate a tasty home-cooked meal, every night of the week. I'm not kidding.

8. She drank beer and smoked. The beer man brought beer in by the case every week. She smoked Camels for fifty years until her lungs were completely shot, then had to give them up. She switched to eating peanuts.

9. She had to be the tough parent. My father wasn't a strong character, so she had to be the enforcer.

10. She got stressed out once and had to take a break at Friends Hospital. We visited her on Sundays. It was hard to see her in there with the crazy folks. She calmed down after a few months and came back home again.

11. She had to do everything after my father died, when he was only 50. Betty did it all after that. She paid the bills, ran her business, raised four kids, and cooked dinners.

12. One time before dinner, she announced that she was going to say grace. We all quieted down. She opened the Bible and read something about a guy who tied his ass to a tree and walked away twenty paces. She had a picture of Jesus on her dresser. I hope he wasn't mad.

13. She planned family trips to far-off places that could be reached by station wagon: Yellowstone, the Canadian Rockies, and Florida. She figured out the whole itinerary months in advance. They were great trips.

14. Later she bought a big RV camper called the Cortez. She actually let us kids take it to California when I was just out of college. We got it stuck in a ditch in Colorado; we

burnt up the brakes in California, and the whole thing caught on fire in Texas. She was brave.

15. She took up smoking pot in the 70's. She didn't want to support criminal activity, so she had to grow her own. She cleaned out the old coal bin, built a false door, and created an amazing secret growing room.

16. She let our rock and roll band practice in the basement. After practice, people hung out in her bedroom, toked up, and listened to James Brown on the stereo.

17. She was a Republican most of her life. Then Bush Jr. came along. That did it for the Republicans.

18. She would always listen if you had a problem. Somehow she understood any bizarre situation you might be in, and had some good advice. I don't know how she did it.

19. She got cancer in her lungs, probably from all those Camel cigarettes. She was hooked up to machines for a while, and then she told them enough was enough. She thanked the doctors for trying, and they unhooked her.

20. On her last day, she wrote my sister a note, and said she was sorry we weren't more like Ozzie and Harriet in our family. She didn't need to worry. She did a heck of a job.

# Life Review

They say that when you are just about to pass away, you do a quick review of your whole life. You see all of your major pluses and minuses. But why wait? It's more relaxing to do it now, while you aren't being run over by a truck.

I wish I had been more heroic. If I were in *It's a Wonderful Life* and the angel gave me a chance to see what the world would have looked like without me, we both might have been shocked. "Well," says the angel, "looks like the world is pretty much the same without you. I'll be darned."

The alarming thing is how many people I almost killed or badly injured, mostly because of lack of attention. I was spacing out, as usual, and I almost creamed around 25 different people. It's a sad realization. Some of the close calls were:

**Arthur White.** We were taking our old tree house apart. Arthur was standing on the ground and I chucked a big board down. It just missed his head. He was upset, and I don't blame him. Arthur took off for Mexico decades ago, and never came back. Some people just disappear from your life, and you never find out where they went or what happened to them.

**Our whole family on vacation.** I had just learned to drive. I took over the wheel while my mother took a nap in the back of the station wagon. I pulled in front of a car trying to pass us. The whole family almost got wiped out. My mother shrugged and went back to sleep. Nothing she could do now.

**Tom on his motorcycle.** My friend Tom was stopped in front of my car on his motorcycle. I drifted forward and pushed him out into traffic. Nobody hit him, and he is still talking to me. A win-win situation.

**Thanksgiving guest.** One Thanksgiving day I was with a group of folks, and we decided to give up eating, go for a walk, and throw a football around. I threw a long pass that almost hit a guy in the face. It was close.

**The burnt match episode.** I was hanging out with my teenage pal in my teenage room, doing my favorite teenage pastime (nothing). I was sitting in a stuffed chair, while lighting matches and dropping them into a hubcap on the floor. You have to keep yourself entertained somehow. Suddenly my friend pointed out that the chair was on fire. He hated to interrupt me, but thought I should know. While I was running around screaming and looking for a bucket of water, he slapped the fire out with his hand, and we went back to listening to tunes on the record player. This friend was the only person I knew who ate frozen hot dogs, with no cooking involved. He just took them out of the pack and crunched away. We all have unique talents.

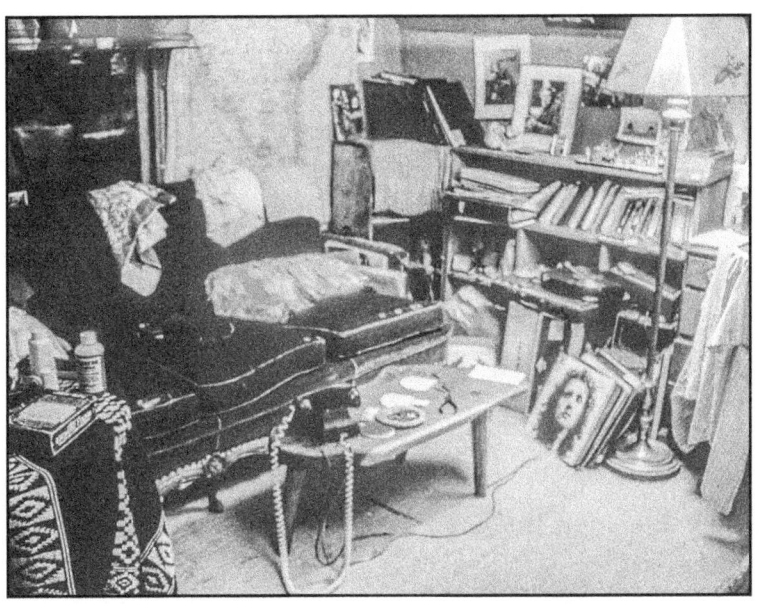

*Yon teenaged bedroom. Better to not burn it down.*

**The flying ski.** This time I was driving my old '68 Falcon, going along on Route 70. I had my cross-country skis lashed to the roof. My lashing skills aren't much better than my driving. One ski came loose, and went flying back into traffic. I pulled over to have a look. The ski was now a pile of splinters with a binding attached, and truck drivers were doing some nifty high-speed swerving. I got out of there in a hurry. I didn't read about any traffic pileups in the news, and no troopers have stopped by to have a chat with me yet. Just to be sure, I took the numbers down off the front of our house.

**The two girls from England.** Carol and I were camping in Colorado in our van. I backed into our site one night, barely missing two girls from England lying on the ground in sleeping bags. I can see the headline now: *"Elderly A-hole from Iowa backs over tourists, Claims they weren't there yesterday, To face charges of womanslaughter and backing up without looking. Asks if they serve any tofu in the slammer."*

**Another guy on a motorcycle.** I was driving (here we go again), talking to Carol, and we were having an argument. Hard to believe, but true. I pulled out in front of a motorcycle, and he had to do the brake and skid thing. He was peeved, but luckily unarmed

And so I almost wiped out a small squadron of innocent humans. Guardian angels may have been involved in saving them. Hopefully angels don't carry grudges (no pockets) and all will be forgiven.

# We Have Been to Europe

Everybody should go to Europe at least once. When you get back, you can say you have been there, and you will have proof. You will have four thousand photos that you took. Nobody will look at these photos, including you, but it is important to take them. Your partner stands in front of the church, and you take the picture. Then you can say, "That's my partner in front of a church in Europe." And people will say, "Wow! When's lunch?"

We have been to Europe, and we have the pictures to prove it. We flew over and back using airline miles, which Carol was able to save up by using her airline credit card for everything, including drinks of water. After ten years of charging, the miles were there. Soon we were there too.

When you fly over to Europe, you fly all night, and you are flying against the sun's direction. This means you lose a lot of hours. They shut the lights off in the plane, and you take a little snooze. After an hour and half, they turn the lights back on again and serve breakfast. They aren't fooling anybody. You haven't had any sleep. You hit the ground in Rome, and you try to do stuff, but you are in a daze.

This is bad timing, because you are wandering right into a group of gypsies and pickpockets who hang around the airport looking for dazed tourists. These people know all kinds of tricks to distract you, like the old throw-the-baby routine. A lady chucks a baby at you, and while you reach up to make the catch, somebody else is lifting your wallet from your pants pocket. It's the oldest trick in the book. I wonder how much the baby gets paid. He is the most important guy in the squad.

Then you have to catch a cab into town. You'll see some seriously tiny cars on the road. Everybody is going really fast, while driving 10 inches apart. Somehow it works.

*Seriously tiny cars. These are normal over there.*

In Europe, the people speak other languages. This is cruel, but true. Over there most people speak at least five languages. Americans only speak one, and that's American—the one true language, the language God speaks. You can look it up yourself in the Bible. If the people don't understand, try hollering. You can barge your way around the world yelling and pointing.

The main thing about Europe that makes it so unforgettable is how much everything costs. How do they live? If you are thinking about dinner for two, they will give you an estimate. It's like having your house painted. We never ate a meal in a restaurant in Europe. All our meals came from take-out windows. That was our only hope.

Pizza makes it all possible, as well as ice cream, except they call it gelato. You point to what you want and make a smiley face. They weigh it on a scale, and charge you some European money. Then you sit by a fountain and eat. We met a nun over there, who said, "Pizza, ice cream, and God. What's not to like?"

The people look sharp in Europe. They don't walk around in sweatshirts with the names of football teams printed on the front. They live on ice cream and pizza, and yet are thin as rails. The Americans, who eat "health food," are all size Jumbo. If you understand how this works, let me know.

The main things to see are the churches. They are everywhere, and they are huge. You say *wow* when you go inside, looking at the art and the spectacular altars. Then you go outside, and there are beautiful fountains. You go from churches to fountains all day long. There are also ancient ruins. A lot of wild cats live in these. Please, don't step on the cats while enjoying the ruins.

You can get around by train. You buy a ticket, just like over here, but there is no authority figure in a uniform to hand it to. You just keep it as a souvenir. Think of it as a free postcard.

Venice is about the most beautiful place you can ever see. The stained glass is to die for, but that would ruin the trip, so you should stay alive. You have to go everywhere by boat. Even the UPS guy delivers his packages by boat. All the buildings are sitting there with their foundations underwater. How this works without the buildings tipping over, I don't know.

Europe should be seen by everybody. Pictures should be taken, and pizza eaten. You won't be sorry.

*How do these buildings survive? There must be a trick to it.*

## Headline News

If you listen to radio in the Midwest, you'll hear things you don't hear on the coasts, such as the funeral announcements. They tell you who crossed over, checked out, and split the scene. Then they say where the service will be held.

They also tell you the lunch menu for the week at the senior center. A lot of tater tots are involved. Maybe we should start practicing eating tater tots now, so our stomachs will be ready. Tater tots are packed with many good things, possibly including food. So we have that to look forward to.

It is a good deal being a senior. You can save a lot of money. Some places in town give you a discount on your pizza. They don't ask for ID, which is kind of sad. One glance is enough. Another place gives you a free soda when you order a pizza. So if you like pizza and soda, you'll like being a senior. Also you can get into the movies at a discount. That's why they call these the golden years.

I have a friend in New York, who I will call Howard, because I don't want Jonathan Tobias to get into trouble. "Howard" did a little research, and discovered that young people actually can't see seniors. We are invisible to them. He found he could walk right past the young ticket takers at movie theaters, and get into any film for free. So the deal keeps getting better and better. Maybe when we hit 90, they'll pay us to go in.

Besides senior and funeral news, the local radio also tells you what happened with the high school sports teams. For example, Melissa Smith had seven kills yesterday. Hopefully this was on the volleyball court, and not at the post office. This is information we can use.

I used to get my news on television. A man named Walter, who was very friendly and honest, told me what had happened that day. I trusted him, because he had no reason to lie. Walter is no longer around, and neither is my TV. The main way I find out what is going on is through the Internet, the place where every crackpot is an expert and vice versa. That's democracy in action.

When the computer comes on, the day's major headline appears on the screen. It might be about a workplace where one particular guy who seemed like a nice enough fellow suddenly flipped and "stood his ground" (shot everybody in sight). His co-workers were shocked. Maybe he was a little peevish at times, but who isn't?

Now that you think about it, he reminds you A LOT of Wally, the guy in the next cubicle, with the wild look in his eyes. Wally has mentioned "going out in a blaze of glory" several times recently. Then he started practicing target shooting in the break room. Whenever you ask him what time it is, he says "the end times." They make some stylish bullet-proof vests these days. Might be worth looking into.

There could also be foreign news, including a report from Beirut on a mysterious car that didn't blow up. The guy parked it, walked away, and nothing happened. He went back a few hours later and it was still sitting there. He tried jiggling the key, he pounded on the battery cables, and he put it in and out of gear; and still nothing. So he took it back to the dealership, where they decided it was an electrical problem. Luckily this was covered by the warranty.

There was a monster headline about a major film actress of our day who had a malfunction with her dress, while she was out in public. It was all documented by a heroic volunteer citizen cameraman. Where would we be without these guys?

This actress suffers from "camera tan." She has had her picture taken so many times that the flashes have permanently tanned her skin. In this particular event, a nipple made a surprise appearance. Can't we be adults about this? No, we can't. I am thinking about contributing to the Save the Dress Foundation. If I don't get involved, who will?

There was another news story, about a guy who had a summer job working as a lifeguard in Ocean City, New Jersey. He sat on a lonely wooden tower, looked at ladies in bathing suits, and developed a serious tan. Then he found out about some illegal activity involving some of the other lifeguards, and he reported it to the authorities. That's right—he was a whistle blower.

# On the Beach

Often you see stories on the Internet news that you just can't believe, but this one topped them all. It was about a guy who found some whale vomit on a beach, and later found out it was worth 50 thousand dollars. I am not making this up. This is not the imagination of the writer. This is *reality*, or "a thing that actually happened."

This whale vomit seems overpriced to me. Who is paying this much for it, and why? Is he a collector? Does he have a fetish, or "thing" for whale vomit? Does he smoke it? I am not here to judge anyone. I am just trying to understand.

How does he feel about cats? I have some excellent samples of cat vomit right here in my house that I am willing to sell if the price is right. I would take 50 thousand bucks for it, as long as the buyer paid for the shipping. I am ready to make a deal.

I never even knew whales threw up. What would make a whale hurl? Maybe some stale plankton? If the plankton was out in the sun, it might have gone bad. Whales eat plankton like we eat French fries, so that could explain it.

Whales are social animals. In other words, they like to party. Sometimes the next day, they don't feel so good. They might heave a little. It's part of whale life they don't show on those TV nature specials. They don't want the children to see that.

A lot of ocean water is polluted, and whales have to drink it, because they can't afford bottled water. So there are probably a lot of whales throwing up on any given day. This is good luck for you, the "entrepreneur." That's a French word for a guy with no job.

You have to study the market, and learn about whale vomit buyers. Where are they? Are there clubs or bars where they hang out? Do they dress and look a certain way? Can you approach them directly if you have some "stuff" they might be interested in? Do they pay cash? Will this transaction be reported, or under the table?

Then there are the tax implications. If somebody gives you 50 G's for some whale vomit, you could end up in a new tax bracket. Thanks to today's miracle economics, the more money you make, the less tax you pay. This is a good deal all the way around, except for the whale.

So how do you get started in the field of whale vomit collection? You need training so you know what you are doing. I looked into it, and they are offering a four-year program in whale vomit at our local community college. They start you off with WV001, **Intro to Whale Vomit**, with Professor Max Peterson. You have to get his book. It weighs a ton, and you need to carry it to class. Life can be hard.

In the second year there is a lot of lab work. You have to be pretty good with a Bunsen burner. Plus they make you take Social Studies. Again, the books are big.

For the third and fourth years, you do field work. Classes are held out on the beach. Mr. Peterson hangs out there, under a red umbrella. He has a big cooler with iced tea in it, but he won't give you any. You can complain, but who will listen to you? You'd have to pay somebody to do that.

In order to graduate you have to write a thesis and defend it. It helps if you know karate. They give you a certificate so you can go right to work. Your friends laughed at you when you started, but who's laughing now? Thomas Edison once said a lot of people don't recognize opportunity when they see it, because it is dressed like whale vomit. He was a smart guy.

Starting a new career is never easy. Years ago the big thing was computer programming, but now all the computers are being programmed by foreign guys who get paid 50 cents a day and sleep sitting up at their desks, so you can't compete with them. But they don't know much about whales. This may be your chance to make it to the big time, the only time that matters.

Everybody has the same dream. It involves a big house, with a sports car in front, a boat out back, and a pogo stick leaning against the side. And then there's you standing on the deck with a drink in your hand, and a big grin on your face. A guy named Roscoe is standing there with a bucket of ice, ready to give you cubes as needed. Go for it. Hit the beach.

## **Altered States**

The 1960's and 70's were a time of experimentation and change. In those days we made many attempts to alter our consciousness. We wanted to go beyond our limited selves and experience something a little more on the cosmic side. Here are some of the techniques we tried:

**The Chair of Destiny.** This was a brown saucer chair that could spin all the way around. One guy sat in it with his legs crossed. Three other guys stood around him to work as facilitators. They started the chair spinning at a pretty good clip, while the subject looked at a psychedelic picture. After 30 seconds, he would stand up and take off running sideways until he crashed into a wall. Hilarity ensued.

**The Darkroom Vision.** My brother had a camera flash that could be flashed repeatedly. We all gathered in his darkened bedroom, held out our arms, and watched as he fired off some flashes. If we moved our arms back, we'd still see them sticking out in front of us. Far out.

**Fast Breathing with Headphones.** I sat on my bed wearing headphones, listening to a record, while breathing really fast through my nose. I got light-headed. That's something.

**The Candle Stare.** The idea is to stare at a candle for as long as possible. Not just any candle. It has to be lit.

**Huff and Puff.** I tried breathing in and out of a paper bag, just to see what would happen. Louise from next door was there to witness the experiment. She was not impressed.

*The author huffs air from a paper bag. Louise is not impressed.*

**The Magic Brownie.** Somebody made some brownies with pot in them. What harm can a few little brownies do? We ate them and went for a nice walk in the park. Then we went back to the house and played some music, which was even better. All of a sudden, there was trouble. The high was too intense. Hospitalization seemed imminent.

I made it as far as the hallway and collapsed on the floor. Luckily the dog came along and licked my face for 15 minutes. That brought me around. Dogs have been trained for these types of emergencies. Watch out for those brownies.

**The Gas Mask.** This apparatus was made out of an old army gas mask that was attached to the bowl of a pipe. The researcher strapped on the mask, and his associates filled the bowl with pot and fired it up. The person always came out a changed man. He would be wrecked, as they say in the towing industry. It was all part of the collegiate experience. My grandparents paid seven grand a year for this.

**Stay High All The Time.** Toke up before any important event, such as a concert, any trip out of the house, or when you can't think of anything else to do. After a while, you are hardly breaking even, and you start to wonder if there is a better way to live your life.

So these were our attempts at altered states. We wanted to break the boundaries and go beyond normal existence. We wanted to be relaxed and happy. Was that asking too much? Yes, it was.

Eventually the experiments were closed down. We went on to live "normal" lives. They can't say we didn't try.

# The Green Falcon

Everybody remembers their first car. Mine was named Falkie. He was a green '68 Ford Falcon. I was 28 years old, and it was high time I had a car of my own. My friend Conrad went with me to check it out. The owner was an older gent, who babied the car and took great care of it. I paid the guy some cash and "took possession," as your lawyer might say if he was stalling for time hoping another hour would go by.

At last, I was a man. In every culture, there are signposts that tell you when you have become an adult. In our case, it happens when you own your first car. It's a beautiful moment.

That Falcon was a good car. It was so basic that I could work on it myself. You young folks out there, you should know that people used to work on their own cars. I bought a box of tools, and I changed the spark plugs and did other repairs. That car had around 15 moving parts, counting the windows, and you could see what all of them did. There weren't any computers involved. You just took out a wrench and fixed stuff. That's the way it was.

Falkie drove me around Philly for a while, to the shopping mall and to the food store, where a person could buy the cheese and bread needed to keep life going for another week. After a while it was time for a change. I needed to head west to San Francisco, to start a new life. I filled that car to the brim with my electric piano, my skis, and some clothes. We started out across the country.

This wasn't going to be a high-speed trip. Falkie didn't go much beyond 60 miles per hour. That was his limit. After that, he wasn't so sure. On Route 80, everybody is going 80, which is how it got its name. So Falkie and I took the two-lane highways, where 60 seems like a normal speed. Along the way we got to see the town squares of America. These are the geeks and nerds that make up our great nation.

Then we got into the Rocky Mountains, where we had a flash mob experience. Those mountains are a lot bigger than they look on the map. I was trying to go over a mountain pass on the way to Steamboat Springs, but my car was in trouble.

My poor old Falcon was gasping for air, like a guy running for the 8:02 local train at the Jenkintown station. It went slower and slower. Honkies (white men with car horns) were lined up behind me. Finally the car wouldn't go any further, and I had to pull off at a rest area. It was mighty distressing. I would have to back up and go halfway across the state to find an easier route.

I was sitting there on a bench, at a scenic overlook, with my head in my hands, moaning and complaining to myself. Why did I ever start this trip? Why is life so hard? Questions with no answers.

Then a bus pulled into the rest area, and a bunch of folks got out and formed themselves into a choir. They broke into a beautiful gospel tune. I looked up at them and the mountain scenery. Life was good again. It wouldn't take very long to drive around this detour. I would make it to San Francisco, land of many restaurants and the ocean. So this flash mob experience really did change my life, at least for that day. You always go back to being yourself again.

I lived for two years in San Francisco, in different apartments, including one where I slept over a hot water heater. I wasn't levitating. There was a wooden platform. During the days I rode the trolley to the downtown area to do extremely boring jobs in banks. So Paradise wasn't everything I thought it would be. Not even close.

Falkie lived for two years in San Francisco. Then he made the long drive back to the Midwest. For a while he had a job in Iowa, as the star of the Green Falcon Driving Service. Somebody made up a cartoon poster, with my special slogan, "Cheep!" We gave people rides to the airport, and they brought their own luggage and insurance. He never broke down on the job, but he was getting old.

Then one day it happened—he reached the end of the line. The mechanic shook his head. There was nothing more he could do. Falkie would never start again. He was taken to the junk yard.

Falkie had a brief life after that. He was towed to the local fairgrounds, where he had fifteen minutes of fame in a monster truck show. A monster truck rolled over him, while people cheered. In the Midwest, this is actually a form of entertainment. I am glad I wasn't there to see it.

Falkie was towed back to the junk yard for the final time. He had a good life, and he always did his best. Skol, Falkie!

*Poster for the Green Falcon Transport Service.*

# Honey Goes Blind

Our cat Honey went blind. She didn't do it on purpose. It just happened. Now she wanders around the house bumping into things. Then she takes a break and has a little snooze. She might not be able to hear either. Where is Anne Sullivan when you need her? We need a miracle worker around the house.

*Honey, the blind Siamese cat, locating her lunch by smell.*

She also isn't that good at hitting the litter box. Sometimes she forgets completely about the box, so we find streams of cat tinkle, to use the technical term, on the floor. We don't see them in advance, so we find them by stepping in them. Then we say a series of bad words and change our socks. I don't know if Honey thinks this is funny.

We never thought she would live this long. We thought she was down to her final weeks on earth. But that was months ago, and she keeps on living. In fact, she seems to be getting stronger. She might keep going like this for years. How many times can we say bad words and change our socks?

One time she got loose and was missing for over a week. We thought she was a "goner," as they say in the funeral business. It turns out she walked down the block, and she made friends with a fellow who restores railroad cars. He has a nice collection of old passenger cars on a railroad siding that he owns.

Most people don't have their own rail siding, but this guy does. People send him train cars from all around the country. He fixes them up, makes sure the wheels are on nice and straight, and he sells them to somebody else. A locomotive backs into his yard and takes them away. Amazing, but true.

 He kept her (the cat) in a cage for a while, and gave her food and water. Eventually we heard she was there, and we went and got her. Now she is back home again, planning her next escape. She probably has a tunnel going under the washing machine. It is all part of the universal desire to escape, to seek out a better life, anywhere but here.

I know what she is going through. I am working on a tunnel of my own, under the dryer. Eventually I hope it goes all the way to Hawaii. It's slow going, and there is a constant problem with moisture leakage. Also, where do you put that much dirt? The neighbors are getting suspicious.

This was a bad year for our cats. A few months ago, Tyke crawled under the back porch and died. I had to retrieve the remains. It wasn't the best of days. A couple of friends came over to give moral support, but they weren't willing to crawl under the porch. That's where they drew the line. The general rule is "you do it because you have to." That's how the universe works. It's all there in the scriptures and in *People* magazine.

Tyke died suddenly and mysteriously. Just a week before, he seemed fine. He had a little cough, but who doesn't? Next thing we knew, he was gone. I had to take the porch apart to get to him. When I crawled under there, I saw that he had captured a bird and parked it next to himself. I know the ancient Egyptians were buried with things they might need in the afterlife. Maybe Tyke had that idea with this bird.

Tyke was just a baby when we found him, mewing pathetically in our back yard. We don't know how such a little kitten ended up on his own, or what happened to his feline family. He lived with us for many years, but never really did trust us. We fed him and took care of him all that time, but he still wondered if it was a trick. He had trust issues.

Ginobili died this year as well. He had a medical problem, but he wouldn't let us take him to the vet. I tried and paid the price of a shredded arm. By the time he was weak enough to be picked up and carried to the car, it was too late. He was named for a famous basketball player from Texas, but Ginobili was from Iowa.

Mrs. Gray also passed away recently from infected teeth and other horrors. It's not always easy being on earth, for cats, people, and even worms. It's a rough planet. A cat's life looks simple, but it might be harder than it looks.

Ms. Fluffy is doing OK, but she is missing a lot of parts. She doesn't have any claws, teeth, or a tail. This is a cat with serious disadvantages in any kind of fighting situation, which is why she sleeps at least 22 hours a day. It is a strict routine. She is a great kitty, she follows the rules, and she knows how to use the litter box. Mostly, she is still alive and purring. We salute Fluffy, and all our kitty cats, present and departed. Meow!

*Fluffy. Her previous owner had her claws removed, not us!*

# All You Can Eat

Fluffy the cat sleeps on my bed at night. She has her own little pillow right by the window, and that is her spot. Everyone needs a spot in this world. In the morning I open the shade and tell her to look, a new day has begun. As proof, I point out that the sun is up, the birds are chirping, and people are driving off to work. She doesn't see it that way. In her opinion, it is all one long continuous day divided into light and dark segments. She will not recognize or celebrate this as a distinct new day. Fine.

Fluffy is always really happy to see me when I wake up, but I have to wonder what this is all about. Is it love or breakfast? Even though Fluffy has lost all of her teeth, she is still eating like a champ. She is always ready for the food bowl.

Like Fluffy, I have barely missed a meal in my whole life. I did try fasting once, for an entire day, and it was weird. How do you divide up your day if there are no meals? How do you know the afternoon has started if there wasn't any lunch? No, this is not for me. Fasting is not normal.

I used to eat heroic amounts of food as a youngster, every chance I got. Mrs. Bell, from two houses down, used to call me "the bottomless pit." I could wipe out her family's groceries for the week, and she'd have to go to Kelso's market to stock up again. That was a little neighborhood grocery store, about the size of a volleyball court.

Mr. Kelso wore an apron, and he did everything in the place—sweep the floor, ring you up at the register, cut the chubby end off of a cow and run it through the slicer. He sold loaves of bread and cartons of eggs. It wasn't a supermarket.

This store was right down the street from our house. We could ride there on our bikes to get a soda and ice cream sandwich, the snack of kings. Mrs. Bell went by station wagon. The dogs traveled on foot, but they rarely went to Kelso's. They had their own lives to live.

I used to consume plenty of groceries at our house as well, but my mother was used to it and stocked way up on everything. Recently I tried to count how many slices of bread I ate every day, and the answer was a lot. (Ten? Is that possible?) This was all white bread. We were not Jewish, Democrats, or from the Ukraine. It was Wonder Bread all the way. I was not gluten-free by a long shot. I lived on gluten, and somehow I survived.

For dinner I had three helpings of everything, and that was just a warm-up. I would have eaten the pots and pans, but my mother needed them for tomorrow. At the same time, they called me "Beanpole" at summer camp because of chronic skinniness. Doctors have tried to explain this paradox, but they are helpless, like turtles flipped over on their backs, their legs waving in the air, their stethoscopes banging against their shells, diplomas framed and nailed to the wall.

One time our family was on vacation, driving across the Midwest in our station wagon. The Midwest is a big flat area we had to cut across to get to the Rocky Mountains and other scenic spots. It was a long hot drive, and we got hungry along the way (law of nature) so we stopped at restaurants. One place specialized in club sandwiches, so that's what we ordered: Six club sandwiches with all the trimmings (toothpicks).

Nobody could finish theirs, except me. I was just getting started. I ate half of my mother's sandwich. Then half of my older sister's. Then my half of my younger sister's. I was eyeing my brother's plate, when he told me to give it up. "Just stop," he said, and he meant it.

There are animals like goldfish that will eat until they die if you give them unlimited food. My brother thought of me as a tall goldfish with glasses. He figured I would keep going until there was an explosion or I keeled over. He was probably right.

**Some fun food facts:**

If you hold your ear up to a glass of Sprite, you can hear the sound of the ocean.

Some restaurants serve a dish called "new potatoes." I like a good bargain, but I would certainly never eat used potatoes.

I'm developing a new food product called "knee macaroni." Investors, make yourselves known.

# The Wyncote Olympics

What does it take to do well in the world? Why do some people succeed and others not so much? What is the secret to getting ahead? It's all a matter of three things: looks, money, and who you know. In other words, three strikes and I'm out. That rule is true on the baseball diamond and in real life as well.

Baseball is the great American game. The last time I gave it a whirl was when I was a school-bus driver. They had a company softball game for all the drivers at a local park one afternoon. I wandered out into left field, my usual locale. I raised my glove to catch a fly ball, and my shoulder popped out of place. I put the glove down and drove back home. That shoulder has never been the same. But, what has?

When you are young, you play games like baseball, basketball and football. You go outside with your friends, choose up sides and play the game. When you get older, you are too old for such nonsense, so you sit and watch grown men play for a million dollars a game. Weird deal, but that's how it works.

We used to play a lot of softball, back in the olden days. We had a small baseball field, known as Hallinger Field, in the bottom half of our property. We couldn't find any corporations to sponsor us, so it was not called Yoo-hoo Stadium or Tastykake Arena. My father was the groundskeeper. There was no lighting. We could only play till it got dark or the game was called on account of dinner. You hardly ever see professional sports events called off on account of dinner.

Our field was pretty small, not regulation by any means. We didn't have pitchers as a skilled position. Usually the batting team pitched to themselves. There were no umpires or uniforms. Almost every hit went into the trees for a home run. It gave you a lot of confidence as a batter.

In the fall, there were touch football games played on the same field. You had to think of a play, and draw it on the ground. Usually the play was "run out for a pass," but it seemed to take a long time to think of that. It isn't rocket science.

Across the street was Kelley's basketball court. The people had to move their cars out of the way, but they didn't seem to mind. In the winter, we shoveled snow off the driveway so we could play. We were dedicated, and frozen fingers weren't going to stop us. You need something to focus on in life, and for many young men, shooting baskets is a good choice.

There were two basic plays. The number *one*, where you shot the ball yourself, or the number *two*, where you passed it to the other guy and he shot the ball. Not that hard to memorize the playbook. How many hours were spent there, working on these two basic plays, with all their variations, no tongue can tell. A good time was had by all.

At the end of the street, was Bell's pool. Yes, they had an actual swimming pool, and they let us go in. They had a diving board, a record player, and a stack of Beach Boys albums. How can you beat that on a hot day in August?

In the basement of our house was the ping-pong table. So many games were played there, all night long, until the sun was just about to come up. Shot after shot, forehand and backhand, with the occasional smash thrown in for good measure. We weren't great players at any of the games. We had energy and time in those days, and that was all we needed.

When we got old enough to drive, we got into car rallies. Somebody would go ahead and plan a secret route. We had to drive all over the place and find hidden treasures and make it back with the best time. This was in the days of 25 cent gasoline, when we could drive all day for the fun of it.

One year we held our own Olympics. All these sports were in it, plus bowling, weightlifting, and archery. There was even a car rally. We had a stopwatch and a scorecard. There were medals for every event, but we all had the same national anthem, so no need to play that. I thought I was going to win, but I didn't. Rudy won. It was a great disappointment, but that's what sports are all about.

## 1973 WYNCOTE OLYMPICS

| | PTS | POS. | EVENT | POS. | EVENT | POS. | EVENT |
|---|---|---|---|---|---|---|---|
| 1] Rudy Kastenhuber | 15 | 1ST | WEIGHTLIFTING-SWIMMING | 2ND | 50 YD. DASH | 3RD | ½ mi. RUN BASKETBALL |
| 2] Pete Molnar | 12 | 1ST | BOWLING | 2ND | BILLIARDS ROAD RALLY | 3RD | ARCHERY |
| 3] Conrad Creighton | 11 | 1ST | ARCH. | 2ND | WEIGHTLIFTING-SWIMMING | | |
| 4] Ken Fretz | 11 | 1ST | 50 YD. DASH | 1ST | ARCH. BOWLING | | |
| 5] Chris Hallenger | 11 | 1ST | PING-PONG BASKETBALL | | | 3RD | BILLIARDS |
| 6] Ted Heller | 9 | 1ST | ½ mi RUN | 2ND | BASKETBALL | 3RD | WEIGHTLIFTING |
| 7] Tom Kern | 6 | 1ST | ROAD RALLY | | | 3RD | 50 YD. DASH |
| 8] Dale Fetterman | 5 | 1ST | BILLIARD | | | | |
| 9] Harry Bell | 5 | | | 2ND | ½ mi RUN | 3RD | PING-PONG SWIMMING |
| 10] Ernie Peters | 4 | | | 2ND | PING-PONG | 3RD | BOWLING |
| 11] Marc Silverberg | 1 | | | | | 3RD | ROAD RALLY |

### RECORDS

| | | |
|---|---|---|
| ARCHERY | 65 PTS | CONRAD CREIGHTON |
| BOWLING | 566 SERIES | PETE MOLNAR |
| SWIMMING | 26.40 SEC. | RUDY KASTENHUBER |
| WEIGHTLIFTING | 200 lb. BENCH PRESS | RUDY KASTENHUBER |
| 50 YD. DASH | 6.2 SEC. | KEN FRETZ |
| ½ MILE RUN | 2 min. 32 sec. | TED HELLER |

*Wyncote Olympics scorecard. (Courtesy Rudy K.)*

## The Five Gottas

Look around you. People are running here and there, going as fast as they can, yelling into their cell phones, and texting with all their might. What is the point behind this whirlwind of activity? What causes it all to happen? It is the five gottas. They are the driving force behind everything that happens in the universe. In order of urgency, they are:

1. Gotta breathe.
2. Gotta take a leak.
3. Gotta have some fun.
4. Gotta get something to eat.
5. Gotta get some sleep.

If you understand the gottas, you understand life. Like so many vital things, this isn't taught in school, but it is important to know. This has been a free educational service brought to you by Accomac Press, the company that cares.

Everybody needs a daily routine. If you do the exact same thing every day, you can relax. You know what to expect. The older you get, the more important the routine is. The idea is to get into a deep rut, never trying anything new or taking a chance, year in and year out. Why make waves?

This is one of the reasons why it was so distressing when our e-mail provider, whose name rhymes with Zahoo, unveiled their new modern format. They were sure it would please everyone and bring pure delight to the unwashed masses, who just got out of bed and haven't had a chance to hit the shower.

Anyway, this company, whose name rhymes with Xahoo, and will remain anonymous for legal reasons, came up with an exciting new format that sucks, to use the colorful idiom from the vacuum industry. Like the check that came from my renter as she was moving to a new location, it is no good. It doesn't function, like a British guy with constipation, which could be just about any British guy. Have you seen what they eat over there?

There is nothing that can be done about it. You can complain; you can be crabby; you can mumble to yourself and shake your fist at your computer. All that does is make them laugh. They can see you through the little camera. They are all rolling around on the floor of their office in Silicon Valley, laughing until it hurts. I'm glad somebody is getting some enjoyment out of this.

I have some canned air on my desk. I use it on my computer keyboard to blow out the dust. Canned air is pretty much regular air, except somehow it got stuck in a can, under pressure, and it can't get out no matter how hard it tries. I know how it feels.

I called my credit card company today to get a few things straight with them. They said they "might" monitor my call for legal and training purposes. Should this make me happy or sad? Then they played some hold music, a song I never heard before, about a guy remembering the good old days of 1978.

He was remembering a day he spent at the lake, which gave me a sudden flashback of a day I spent at the lake, many years ago. I was with some friends. We were driving around and toking up, because that's pretty much all we did in those days.

Somehow we ended up by a lake, and then we were actually in it, swimming around. It was dark out, and we were swimming in the nude. There were some ladies there also swimming nude, and we were all pushing around a giant tree trunk in the water. On the far shore there were some dinosaurs made out of concrete. After a while we got in our car and drove home. That's all I can remember.

A few years ago I asked my friend Bud about this event and what he remembered, because I thought he came along on that trip. He remembered it exactly like I did. We don't know where this place was, how we got there, who the ladies were, or most of all—if they are still naked. But it must have happened, because two guys don't have the same dream except in horror movies, and I'm pretty sure we don't live in a horror movie. Or do we?

Not long after that, Bud had his famous lottery dream.

# Bud's Lottery Dream

Bud had a dream one night. He dreamed that his brother was standing outside on the lawn, holding up a sign with some numbers on it. When he woke up the next morning, he was sure they were lucky lottery numbers, and he told his friends at work the story. His friends all played those numbers that day, and they were indeed the winning numbers. Some of them won nice sums of money. We are waiting for Bud to have another dream, but it's hard to perform under pressure.

The world has changed a lot in the past 50 years. When I was a little kid, only poor people went on strike. They were transit workers, street cleaners and trash collectors. Also celery men, steam inhalers, roustabouts, and the Union of Floor, Fruit and Bikini Waxers local 54. Now only millionaire athletes go on strike. It's some kind of new rule they passed. Once again, we have made progress.

In today's world, a decent athlete makes 50 million a year plus incentives to catch a ball, but it's not really enough. How is he going to keep all his SUV's shined? Is he supposed to drive around in a dusty SUV? That would be cruel. He can't get by on 50 million a year, and neither can anybody else.

That's why I never play the lottery until it gets up to at least 400 million bucks. Otherwise, what's the point? You hear about some clown winning 50 million in the lottery, and you have to laugh. What can you do with that? You buy one decent yacht, and hire a crew of 25 guys with matching uniforms, and your 50 million is toast. You haven't even gone out to sea yet. You are still sitting there in the harbor, with your deck shoes and your new cap, and you are feeling pretty good about how life is going, and then Jamison interrupts you.

He knows how much you hate to be interrupted, so this must be big trouble. He says begging your pardon sir; and you say yes go on Jamison, what is it? And Jamison says, it's the bank balance sir. It has gone minus, sir.

Can't be, you say. There are millions in there. Stop blathering and go below, and finish making the clam chowder. I had those clams flown in yesterday from Sweden. The clams got wise to what was going down, and they started a revolt, and the whole kitchen was in an uproar. The lobsters got in on the act. We had to call in extra troops from the upper decks. Almost lost the whole ship. Now you are telling me we are out of money. Talk sense, man.

But Jamison sticks to his story. Look for yourself sir, he says, and points to the gangplank, where a steady stream of guys in sailor uniforms are all heading for the dock, with their duffel bags over their shoulders. They are abandoning ship, like mice during a cheese shortage. This is why you need hundreds of millions, just to break even. This is not getting ahead. This is just surviving.

Yes I remember the 1960's. In those days, there were people who called themselves "futurists." They predicted that the biggest problem in the future (what we now know as "now") would be boredom. There would be so much free time that people wouldn't know what to do with themselves. Work would only take a few hours a week. We'd spend our days doing flower arranging and learning the correct way to butter French bread (hold it with your left hand, butter with the right, but you knew that already).

Well those futurists were a little off. Will they give us refunds on all the books we bought? Not likely. They are all in Tahiti, living in houses on stilts, so floods won't bother them.

Meanwhile, I met another guy who had a lottery dream. He said a swan flew up in his face and spoke to him, saying "Seven forty eight, is it too late?" while flapping its wings intensely. The fellow was sure this was a message from the other side (Camden), and these were lucky lottery numbers. An angel or somebody up there was looking out for him, and had given him a tip from the great beyond. This was his lucky day.

He put a pile of money on those numbers, but they weren't the winning set. They weren't even close. Not one number was right. You have to be careful, because sometimes swans don't know what they are talking about.

## Of Mice and Women

There is a big mouse problem this year. No, it is not high unemployment among mice, or that they can't get health insurance, or that they are scampering around on their wives.

The problem is they are coming into our house in great numbers. This could mean it will be a bad winter. Mice can sense these things. They know snow and ice are on the way, and they decide to move into our house and make themselves at home. Why freeze? Why shiver? This is how they look at it.

Our house isn't much, but it is heated, with food and water available. For a mouse it is paradise, the land of plenty, and El Dorado. There are no serious predators. There is Fluffy the cat, but she has no teeth and no claws. Not much of a threat there. What's she going to do, read bad poetry to them?

I have a Facebook friend in Philly who is also having a banner mouse year. They are coming into his house in record numbers, and leaving in a lifeless state. He photographs them as ex-mice, and posts the pictures on line. He has his own way of catching them. It has something to do with a bucket of water that the mice fall into. They can only swim so long, and then, so long.

We wouldn't mind being the hosts if they didn't leave little poops everywhere. This includes on mixing bowls, the cutting board, and the cast iron pot. They don't care. Nothing is sacred to them.

They don't respond well to toilet training. Just getting them to show up at class is a major headache. They have short attention spans and very little patience for learning new habits. If it was good enough for their pappy, it's good enough for them.

We had to get rid of them. We couldn't stand wiping off our popcorn bowls before using them. They always had a layer of mouse doots inside. Who wants to live like that? Hardly anyone, especially Carol, she keeps saying.

The problem is, we are wimps. The mice are so cute that we can't stand killing them. So we got a live trap, and Carol started catching some mice. You put some peanut butter in there, and they wander in to have a bite, and they can't find their way out. Simple enough.

This happened to me in Las Vegas once. I went into dinner at the Rio, in what could be the world's largest buffet. You could barely see from one end to the other. The Italian and Chinese sections were actually in different counties. At the end of the meal, I couldn't find my way out of the casino. These places don't have windows, so you can't orient yourself. They design it that way so you will wander around for hours and then start playing the slots just for something to do. There are Midwestern tourists who have been stuck in there for years, living on Sprite and pretzels. Don't let it happen to you.

So the mice are trapped, like highly qualified women in dead-end jobs. Now what? You have to take the trap, with the mice inside, and release them back into the wild. This is called catch and release. It works on trout, mice, and dolphins. The idea is to set them free, and then they march resolutely into the sunset to begin new lives.

We tried to find suitable places where young mice might be able to establish themselves and make a go of it. We looked for a quiet area with some corn or soybeans growing. Carol tried to put them near a factory or any building where they might find lodging and "shelter from the storm."

She also made up a supply package for them, including a few snacks, and some bits of cloth that could be used for bedding. A lot of the mice didn't want to leave the trap. You could see the whiskers twitching and the nose wrinkling. They knew this was a bad deal. Some of these mice were youngsters. They didn't know much about hunting and gathering. They had never been out on their own. It's scary, as we all know.

I wonder if it really is going to be a harsh winter. The mice could be wrong. The caterpillars are supposed to know these things as well, but take a good look at caterpillars. Do they look like meteorological scholars? I'm not sure they even know if they are facing forward or backward. *Please, no letters from the caterpillar anti-defamation league.*

## Two Dogs Saved My Life

One time two dogs saved my life. I was taking these pups out for a walk in San Francisco, so they could do their business (they are in the pooping industry). My friend Jeff was out for the day, and so I was walking his two Irish setters.

Jeff had been my roommate in college. We had lived in an old building in New York City called the Brittany Hotel, on the 15th floor. The elevator call button didn't work, so we had to scream the number of our floor. This got the elevator man's attention, and he would come and pick us up. It worked fine, as long as we could wake the guy up.

Sometimes we played volleyball in Washington Square Park, which was a big source of amusement in those days. Also we took German class together, which I thought might be fun. We could study together and learn something new.

There was nothing fun about it. I studied for hours, failed the course, and only learned one German word. The word was "geschwindigkeitsbegrenzung," which is German for speed limit. That one is stuck in my memory bank for the rest of my life. Maybe it will come in handy someday.

Jeff came to my family home in Philly one weekend, to meet my friends and family. It was a good visit, except my grandfather made a remark about Jewish folks that Jeff didn't care for, being a Jewish folk himself. My grandparents didn't like most ethnic/racial/political groups, so Jeff wasn't alone in being criticized.

I visited Jeff's family home one weekend, in the suburbs of New York. His father owned a string of movie theaters, including some showing adult movies. This was in the early 1970's, the time known as the Golden Age of Adult Cinema. In other words, there were dirty movies being shown in every town. We saw one, and it was memorable.

At that time, Jeff was going out with a girl who came from one of the richest families in New York. Her family owned a summer house in Connecticut, right next to Paul Newman's house. I was there once, but didn't see Paul raking the leaves. I did get a few twigs from Paul's hedge, which I might try to sell on eBay someday when I need the cash, which by an amazing coincidence, is today.

We stayed in touch, and both ended up moving to San Francisco. This one evening I was watching his two setters from Ireland. Call them Mike and Pat. I was walking the streets, when I saw a park off in the distance and headed toward it. What I forgot is, when you are in the city, all of a sudden you can be in the wrong part of town, and you might be in trouble.

The park was quiet, with no toddlers or tots in sight. Some teenage guys came up to me and asked me for the time, but I don't think they had appointments they were worried about. They weren't trying to catch a plane. It was a conversation starter and ice breaker. Things went downhill fast after that. They all got around me, in a menacing kind of way. The time for talking was done. It was time for me to do something, but I'll be darned if I could think of what it might be.

Just then Mike and Pat came bounding up. They were happy to see the young fellows, and they jumped up on them looking for pats and games. The guys freaked out a little, and jumped back.

I took a step away from them. Then I started to jog. Then I was running as fast as I could go, down the streets of San Francisco. My three friends were running behind me. The dogs were loping along with us. This was one of their best walks ever.

I kept up a pretty good pace for a number of blocks, but the young guys stayed right with me. The dogs had no problem keeping up. Every now and then I would yell something like "Help" or "I'm being chased" to pedestrians, but they weren't sure what to do. It was an awkward time.

Finally the guys veered off on a side street, and the pups and I ran back to Jeff's house. We let ourselves in the door, where we all drank water and got our breath back. I had a cup of tea, but the dogs took their water cool. Then we had a rest and thought about what had happened and what might have been. I think those dogs saved my life.

## **The Rooming House**

Everybody has to pay the bills somehow (unfortunate federal law), and this is why I entered the exciting world of Real Estate Investment. I own a big rooming house with six bedrooms in it. When I bought it, the seller jumped up in the air and clicked his heels, like people do in car commercials. When I saw that jump I knew I was in trouble.

One time a lady renter had some friends over and they decided to stab a young fellow to death, right in her room. Somebody went up to see what was going on, and he saw a stabbing in progress. Blood was everywhere, except where it was supposed to be, in the victim's body. What a mess.

The young guy was able to escape. The police came and arrested the "suspects" and strung up yellow tape. All the neighbors came out to gawk and talk, and we had a nice chat about stabbings and the weather and stuff. The rest of the renters went to the police station to testify about what they had seen. I went down there with them, and we all hung out in the police lobby.

The police lobby is a nice enough place. There are posters on the wall, describing different drugs that you might not want to try. Also they have lists of people who are sex offenders and where they live, so you can point at them and laugh. I brought the renters some burgers for dinner, with all the trimmings (catsup).

Later the house opened back up, and the renters went back to their rooms. The guilty trio had to stay in jail. The motive was robbery, but the victim probably didn't have twenty bucks to his name. I don't think this caper was very well thought out.

For me, this whole episode has been a big wakeup call from Mother Nature.

"Hello, is this Chris?"

"Yeah, it is. Who's this?"

"Mother Nature."

"What's up?"

"Listen, you really need to sell that rooming house." And she is right about that. There have been so many characters and events there over the years, including:

**Mr. Peepers.** He was an older gentleman who took up the habit of peeping in his later years. He drilled holes in the walls. He lurked at people's windows. He followed one lady right into the bathroom. Did he think she wouldn't notice?

**The stolen car.** One lady stole another lady's car, and took off for Chicago. She had an appointment there, with destiny.

**The stolen stuff.** One guy rented a lot of expensive equipment from Rent-A-Center. Then he quit his job, loaded all the equipment in his car, and drove out of town to start a new life.

**Where's my ceiling?** One time I took a peek into a lady's room, and noticed that the drop ceiling was missing. She said she took it apart because she was looking for something up there.

**Where's my rug?** I glanced into a guy's room, and noticed that the rug was missing. This was a wall-to-wall rug that I had purchased at Menards. He said it was giving off bad vibrations.

**Where's my bed?** One guy moved out and took the bed with him. Luckily the police helped me out and pounded on the door of his new place. It's amazing what some police pounding can do. The bed reappeared at my rooming house, as if by magic.

**I'm sorry; I just don't feel like paying rent.** One fellow seemed actually insulted that he was asked to pay rent. Eventually the sheriff was called in.

**The lawsuit.** One time I waited half a year for a lawsuit to be settled, so a guy could get his rent money. There never was a settlement. Should I have been surprised?

**The gent with the tent.** One man left all his stuff in his room and went to live in a tent in the local park, probably for some good reason. I had to put his stuff out on the curb.

**Wash the dern dishes.** The dishes, like the Lord's will, must always be done. Try telling that to the folks in the rooming house. Good luck with that.

# The Black Couch

Scientists say that the saddest sound in the world is the sound of the drums when you are walking towards a high school football game. You can hear them from far away, beating a staccato tattoo. You think they will sound better the closer you get, but it doesn't happen. They also say that food, relationships, and jokes all tend to go stale. It has something to do with oxidation.

You have to keep yourself going somehow. In the process, you can end up doing strange activities that make no sense. These activities can be repellant, annoying, illegal, boring, dumb and/or tragic. There's not much you can do about it.

For example, I spent two days on a job in Ottumwa, Iowa putting white coating on a roof. The idea is to keep it (the roof) from leaking. The building is in a dicey area. There are pawnshops across the street, where you can sell anything you managed to steal that day to buy yourself some drugs. They (pawnshops) buy guitars, tools, bikes, and jewelry—surely you can steal some of those. You have to get out there and make something of yourself.

It's actually pretty nice up on the roof. There is a great view of the Des Moines River. Birds are circling around looking for a fish who might be swimming close to the surface. Next thing he knows he is stuck in some effing talons, being carried off to a distant nest where he has been invited to dinner, and his whole day is shot. People are walking by the river trying to relax and lose weight, but not having much luck. Trains are going back and forth on the tracks. These are coal trains, over a mile long. They dig up a mountain in Wyoming and ship it east to be burnt up in a big fire in Ohio, so a guy in New York City can turn his TV on. We are all proud to be on the grid.

I just realized I don't know one living relative in my family, except my sister. All other relatives have either moved away or died, maybe both at the same time. Moving can kill anybody.

I helped a guy move out of his apartment recently. This wasn't his idea. It was an eviction. His landlord is a friend of mine, and I was there to help move his belongings out to the street. There were three sheriffs there with uniforms, guns, and badges; the whole ten yards. (Why not go for the first down?) The guy tried to talk his way out of it, but the sheriffs weren't listening. He had to stand aside while we cleared out his things.

His place, like so many other places, was full of what you might call "junk" in the vernacular of the salvage yard industry, which is a pretty good business to go into. There are always new products being made, and eventually they get old and break down, and become junk. If you have some land with a fence around it and a crane, you could add this stuff to your pile.

Possessions were plentiful in this pad: pillows and blankets, a jar of coins, some naughty magazines, and a huge television set that filled one whole wall. I have noticed as a landlord that the poorest people have better TV's and phones than I do, and yet on the first of the month they say they couldn't possibly pay the rent now. Tomorrow is no good either. Why don't I come back in a couple weeks, when things might be better? They are going through a rough patch at the moment. Also, they are busy playing violent video games with the kids.

I rented to one guy who was a peace activist. He traveled all around the country advocating for peace among men. At night he spent untold hours in his living room playing shoot-em-up video games with his brother. They tried to mow each other down with machine guns, and the blood went flying. It was all in good fun.

Anyway, we did finally move all the guy's things out to the curb, including the big black couch. It took some brute force to get it out the door. How did the couch end up in this place? We know that there are two different kinds of couches in the world: new and used. Personally, I have never bought a new couch in my life, and probably never will.

Somebody must buy new couches, and we praise and honor them for starting the chain going. A couple goes to a showroom and picks one that matches their interior (their house, not their bodies). The salesman says they have made an excellent choice, but he is trained to say that.

# Hamstring Muscles

Sometimes you can start a new chapter of your life. All it takes is the desire for change, a little luck, a few good ideas, and a nice inheritance from your rich uncle Fred, bless his soul.

Some people believe that the secret of life is to think positive thoughts. If you think you are rich, you will be rich. For proof, they asked a bunch of wealthy folks, and sure enough, they all thought they were rich.

When I turn my computer on, I always take a look at the sports news: who tackled whom, who made the winning shot, and who was injured. A lot of the guys have problems with their hamstring muscles.

Hamstrings are among the most humorous of the muscle groups, not because of being injured, but because of their name. Why were they called "hamstrings" to begin with? The answer will shock and amaze you.

Jacob Hamstring and his wife Ethel lived in a cottage in Bavaria in the mid 1900's. They were a simple couple. Ethel wrote poetry and canned tomatoes, but not at the same time. Jacob played for his local football team, the Bavarian Eagles. They were having a good season, until Jacob pulled this odd muscle in the back of his leg. "Hey Hamstring," somebody yelled to him, "what's the matter with your leg?" A local newsman was there and thought the comment was funny, so he printed it as a caption with a shot of Jacob limping off the field.

Fast forward a few decades. A man named John Chesterton was in the local library, "doing research" on old Bavarian customs. OK, he was playing on-line chess on the free computer. But he liked to tell people he was doing research. Nobody looking at him could tell the difference. This is the beauty of computers, and why everybody needs one.

On his way out the door, John Chesterton noticed an old-time photo called "Hamstring's Out" that was taken in Bavaria in the 1900's, but he didn't think much about it.

Fast forward 10 minutes. Laura Jenkins was in her kitchen in northern California, making a tofu sandwich. It tastes better than it sounds. She looked out the window and saw her boyfriend John Chesterton coming up the walk, hiding a chicken sandwich wrapper in his coat, and eating a breath mint. Her first novel, called *The Reluctant Vegetarian* was dedicated "to Johnny C, with hopes that he will wake up someday before it's too late." He never got the hint. To tell you the truth, he never read the book. Not many people did.

Fast forward a minute. John came in the door, and said "Hi honey," which is what he always said. She said "Hi honey," right back at him. "Want some tea?" she asked, pointing at the tea, which was steep. It was on an angle, and it was expensive.

John said sure he wanted some tea. A light breeze was blowing past the orange tree. The sunlight was streaming in through the windows of the cottage. There are worse places in the world to live than Northern California.

John worked as plant waterer on a pot ranch, and he cleared half a million bucks every growing season. That's why he could take off all winter and hang out in the library. He used to be poor, but thanks to the Medical Marijuana Miracle, he isn't poor anymore.

The pot that he grows is only for people with certain medical problems such as difficulty in getting things done, problems with falling asleep or being awake, not knowing what fibromyalgia is, can't or won't do the Peppermint Twist, lingering shame about something seen on TV, difficulty breathing while underwater, having double vision or other tunes by Foreigner, delusions of tiny, and other serious conditions. The guidelines are very strict.

John turned to pick up his cup of tea, but he felt a sharp sensation. "Ow," he said, reaching for the back of his leg. "I think I pulled something."

# Watching for Fires

I heard about a job opening at the local senior home, watching for fires. You walk around the building and make sure there aren't any fires. That was the job description. How hard could this be? This was something I could do. This was my lucky day, the nirvana that spiritual seekers strive for, the magic bus the Who sang about, the goal that soccer players dream about: a job where you don't actually do anything.

I am supposed to be retired now, winding down from my career, and heading off to Florida for the big shuffleboard tournament. But I need to keep looking for jobs, thanks to not having had a career. I read in the paper that this is a new fad. Instead of retiring, people keep working "till they drop." So at least I am keeping up with the times.

I had to go to a temp agency to get hired. I filled out an application and I peed into a cup, just to show I could do it. When I said I was finished (the application) a lady in the next office yelled out "You're hired. Can you start tomorrow?" She couldn't even see me. All she knew was that I was alive and breathing. A lot of jobs I have done were like that. As long as I was alive and breathing, I was qualified.

So I went to the place and got trained. That took around five minutes. The sprinkler system had failed, so somebody had to walk the halls to make sure nothing was on fire. I bought some padded shoe insoles to save my feet. On the plus side, there were ten minute rest breaks when I sat in a storage closet and worked on my Sudoku skills. I should have become a Sudoku genius, but the more I practiced, the worse I got. Why?

This place had a beauty parlor for the residents. The ladies liked having their hair done, even if it was silver. And there was a soda shop with an ice cream machine, with pictures from the 1950's. I could have a cone any time I wanted, including the famous vanilla and chocolate swirl. How much was I going to weigh when the job was over?

I met some nice young folks who worked on staff there. One lady lived out in the countryside, near the Amish people. One night she saw an Amish horse and buggy parked by a store. The buggy was rigged with a boom box and subwoofers, with rap music blasting out of it. An Amish kid came out of the store carrying a case of beer and a box of condoms. He was ready to party that night, Amish or not.

The seniors were very friendly. A lot of them used walkers because falling is a big problem. Once a week a woman came in and played old songs on the organ. The residents watched basketball games on the big TV screen. After dinner, cards were played. It was a cozy scene.

I talked to a few of the residents. One lady had gone to school in a one-room school house. There were only three kids in her class. She said it was a very good education, and the older kids helped the younger ones. It seemed normal at the time.

One gentleman was a survivor of the Pearl Harbor attack. Somehow he didn't get blown up. Another guy was a bomber pilot in World War II. He bombed Japan to get them back for Pearl Harbor. Later his son married a Japanese lady, and he made peace with the Japanese people. That's how it works with our country. One day we at war with somebody and bitter enemies, and after a few years we are best friends.

I heard one group of ladies talking, and they said the hardest thing about being in a home like this is not being able to make your own decisions. If you feel like having a pizza, you can't. You have to eat what is being served. Then there is the really sad wing, with residents who can't remember anything or take care of themselves. The end of life can get pretty tough.

It is a strange deal getting old. These people all used to play games and ride bikes. Later they got married and had kids, and did jobs. You have to wonder if any of them ever did a job as stupid as this one. We have our doubts.

When I was a kid there was a lady on our block named Old Lady Reginer. She yelled at us not to ride our bikes too fast. I never realized she was an actual person like the rest of us. I thought she was Old Lady Reginer all her life. Now I am kind of elderly myself. I wonder if kids on my block call me Old Man Hallinger. That reminds me—I should go yell at them. They are riding their bikes pretty fast.

# Memorial for the Dog

I took a trip to the east coast to have a memorial gathering for my brother David "Dog" Hallinger. He was also known as the Pooch, the Pup, and the Hound. He had four dogs living with him in his house in Oregon. They ranged in size from jumbo to tiny, and they all piled on his bed with him to sleep or watch TV. He liked watching the old shows on TV, including *McHale's Navy, The Patty Duke Show*, and *Rin Tin Tin*.

Back in his prime, Dog was a good photographer and movie cameraman. He worked on films like *Top Gun, Ghostbusters*, and the immortal *Weekend at Bernie's II*. He filmed a music video with Robert Palmer, and he said Robert P was a great guy. He shot a movie with James Coburn, and told him that the Hallinger brothers were big admirers of the *Our Man Flint* movies, which amused Mr. Coburn. He rode in a small plane to a film shoot with Audrey Hepburn, and reported that she was just as nice in person as she was on the movie screen.

My brother made his own documentary about the underground filmmaker George Kuchar called *The Comedy of the Underground*. (Copies are available on the website chrishallinger.com.) George made hundreds of videos with titles like *The Naked and the Nude, A Tub Named Desire*, and *Tootsies in Autumn*.

My brother liked traveling. He went to Mexico for one year of college. He took trips to South America, traveling around by thumb and by bus. For a while he was a guide in the Amazon rainforest, taking gringos by canoe to see healing shamans.

He also liked to build things. He bought a funky old building in Newport, Oregon and turned it into the Sail Inn Cafe, with a dining patio looking out on the harbor. In his younger days he was chief architect of a five-story tree house that was furnished with bunk beds and a full-sized couch. We have to wonder how he hauled that couch up there without anybody getting killed.

He sure had a lot of girlfriends in his life, always more than one at a time. Even if he had a steady lady partner, he had one night off a week to see his girlfriend "on the side." Valentine's Day was very complicated and stressful for him. Even in his last days he was still sending emails to "girlfriends" in the Philippines.

He also liked to shop for bargains. Costco was his favorite place in the world, and he would drive for half an hour to get 50 cents off something. He was a unique character, and had his own way of talking and naming things. He hated the word "hashtag." As far as he knew, it was just a pound sign. I never heard him say a curse word in his life.

He went into a slump in his last years, and spent a lot of time in the house watching TV with his pups. He ended up in jail for DUI and other bad initials. While in jail he had trouble swallowing, and then he couldn't eat at all. The authorities thought he was faking, so it took a long time to get medical help. When he finally got to the hospital, they found out he had cancer, and by that time it was very advanced. He was allowed to go free, so the state wouldn't be stuck with his medical bills.

Then his life was all about hospital appointments and treatments. He did the dreaded chemo and radiation routines. He had a feeding tube installed so he could get some nourishment. He said it was like a sword sticking him all the time. I hung out with him while he got his treatments and made mashed potatoes and ice cream for him. My sister came and we had some good family time together. After a few months, they told him his cancer had spread all over, and there was nothing more to be done.

Even though he could barely get out of bed, he decided to take a last-ditch trip to Ecuador, to see the rain forest and the healing shamans one final time. He did enjoy the scenery, but it was too late for any healings. He had to fly home early, and he was rushed into the hospital. He only lived a week after that.

My brother lived in Oregon, but he still had a lot of old friends from the Philadelphia area, the land of hoagies. That's why we gathered there for his memorial. Some people there knew him from elementary school days, when he founded a group of friends called "The Pro Club." People still have his photos hanging up on their bedroom walls. I always admired my brother's ability to be creative, to be himself without being afraid, and to go wherever life led him. I miss the Doggie.

# Dog's Life in Photos

*David H as a little kid, on the couch.*

*His first set of wheels.*

*With step-daughter Colleen, in Oregon.*

*He had an actual horse.*

*With his beloved Little Boy.*

*His photo of young folks in the Andes playing Frisbee for the first time.*

*His photo of a pup in Ecuador.*

*Photo he took at a pow wow near his house.*

*One last trip to the Amazon, in Tena, Ecuador.*

# The Pilgrimage

My brother called me "Kat" when we were little kids, and the nickname stuck. It was spelled with a "K" because it was inspired by a certain candy bar that will not be named here for legal reasons (Kit Kat). I had to get back at him, so I called him "Dog." That was all I could think of.

Dog had a knack for making up nicknames for people and animals. He also had an imaginary place that he invented called "Toast Land," where a person named Mack lived. I'm not sure what Mack did for a living or what Toast Land was like, but it seemed like a real place to me.

My brother was a cameraman, so he lived in Los Angeles for a while. My grandmother needed a new home at the end of her life, so she bought a house in L.A. for both of them to live in. He was the only one in our family who could talk to her, so they became housemates.

Later there was a legal fight about some work on the house that wasn't done right. The workers settled the case by giving my brother a collection of hand-painted cartoon cells. Apparently in California cartoon cells can be used in place of regular money.

Later I inherited some of the cartoons. One was of Popeye the Sailor, and he ended up in my basement, hanging over the workbench, which has the word "work" in it, but don't let that fool you. It's just a big pile of junk on a table.

That whole basement is full of junk. You can tell a lot about a person by looking at his basement. It is like looking into his subconscious. There's a lot down there you'd rather not see. Better to stay away.

One day there was a flood in my basement. Coolers were floating around. So were cat litter boxes, cat poo and pee, good heavens it was all floating around in a toxic soup. This is where the Roto Rooter man came in.

The basement door, to be exact. He dragged his rooter machine down the stairs, and he did his roto thing in the floor drain. It cleared suddenly, like a bathtub that had been unplugged. In a few minutes all the water was gone.

Those guys make good money. The drain was cleared in 15 minutes, and the bill was 200 bucks. These are brain surgeon rates. This seems like a good gig, but the guy has to stand in poo and pee to do the job. Plus he is operating an electric machine while standing in water, which is a couple degrees of danger beyond insane. There is always a catch.

As he unplugged his machine, he noticed the Popeye cartoon hanging on the wall. He had an interesting story to tell about Popeye, and the town of Chester Illinois, a small town on the

Mississippi river, not too far from here. This is the hometown of Popeye the Sailor.

EC Segar was born in that little town. Later he went on to draw the comic strip *Popeye*, and he based some of the cartoon characters on local people. For example, Popeye was based on a fellow named Frank "Rocky" Fiegel, who was a town tough guy. The spinach part never happened.

Olive Oyl was based on a local lady named Dora Paskel, who ran a shop and wore her hair in a bun. Even Wimpy was based on a real person. You couldn't make this stuff up.

This Roto Rooter man happened to be driving along the Mississippi River, when he came to the town of Chester. He stopped in to check it out. He saw statues of Popeye and his pals all over town. He made a day of it, and he was glad he did.

He recommended that I go there myself, as a pilgrimage and a journey of discovery. Hindus go the Ganges, Muslims go to Mecca, and I want to go to the birthplace of Popeye. It is calling me. Someday I will make it to Chester, Illinois.

So I have made a new addition to my bucket list. It comes right after "Visit all the beaches and buffets in the world." Then right after the Popeye Pilgrimage comes "Shoot skeet with Jimmy Fallon." It's an impressive list.

## First Openly Gay Tuba Player

Whenever I talk to people, they lose interest pretty fast, and those silent gaps can get awkward. Luckily there is Facebook, full of slightly amusing events and pictures, like the story of Frankie F, the world's first openly gay tuba player. Frankie plays tuba with the London Midtown Symphony Band, and he is a sensation on the tuba, but when he "came out" everybody wished he would go back in again. It's like the big Hetero Pride parade they just had a few weeks ago. Nobody even showed up.

I have always wanted to go to London. My dream is to have fish and chips for lunch. I don't care about the Tower, the Clock, the Globe Theater, or the Royal Family. I just want to go to a fish and chips joint. Maybe I could ask Roger Daltrey to pass the ketchup. That's my dream. Do they have ketchup over there?

If you want to get anywhere in this world, you have to start by taking out a big loan, some amount you could never pay back, and then go off to college and get a room in a dorm where you live with crazy people. After four years of this they give you a degree so you can make some money. It all makes sense. I'll admit it—I have lived in college dorms myself.

I lived in a dorm in Iowa for one year. A lot of the guys in our dorm had nicknames. There was a guy called Newark because that's where he was from. Another guy was called Moose. He was a lineman on the football team. Moose used to work for the Nebraska Highway Department, and he claimed he once saw a worker fall into the highway-making machine, and the poor devil was minced up and became part of Route 80. This is how the story went. Thinking back on it now, I have doubts.

Then I went to New York City, and lived in a big hotel/dorm with some other NYU students. I had the maximum hippie hair and outfit allowed by law. One time a busload of tourists was stopped beside me, and the announcer was telling everybody to look to the starboard side to see a genuine hippie. People were pointing and taking pictures. I wonder if I am still in a scrapbook somewhere in Indiana.

I still remember a certain coffee shop in New York. I passed it every day on my way to class. People hung out there, drank coffee, and read the paper. You're allowed to read the paper at breakfast, which is a good rule and makes breakfast the most relaxing of all the meals.

Coffee shops are a big fad now. But way back in the 1950's, there were places called soda fountains, manned by young fellows known as soda jerks. The customers sat on revolving stools so they could spin around while waiting for the jerk to make their sodas.

Soda fountains have all disappeared. Where have they gone? To find out, I went right to the source. I decided to interview God.

He has a big office with wood paneling. His secretary buzzed me in, which was a pleasant sensation.

God agreed to a short interview. He/she is busy, and time equals cash. I figured I'd start with a few pleasantries, so I asked how his wife and family were doing. He said he wasn't married, the whole creation was his family, and it was doing OK. Then we got down to the tacks made of brass.

Me: "So, what happened to the soda fountains and jerks? And most of all, is there any point to life on earth?"

G: "**Funny you should ask.**"

He went on to say: "**Things are happening the way they are supposed to. Don't worry so much. You are doing fine the way you are. Don't be too critical of people you meet, because everybody is doing the best they can. Nobody wants to mess up. In times of confusion, the important thing is to follow your own inner guidance. Don't be afraid to be yourself. The answers you need are all there in your heart.**"

That was the end of the interview. Time was up. I was shown the door, which I had already seen on the way in. I bought a newspaper, and the headline said that times were tough everywhere and the whole planet was burning up to a crisp. On the plus side, a guy scored a lot of points in a basketball game.

Then I ran into somebody that I used to know in the old days. He said he was glad to see me, but he might have been lying.

CPSIA information can be obtained
at www.ICGtesting.com
Printed in the USA
BVHW031735120620
581249BV00004B/118